MEN
& STRESS

MEN

Dr Charmaine Saunders

& STRESS

HarperCollins*Publishers*

HarperCollins*Publishers*

First published in Australia in 1997
Reprinted in 1998
by HarperCollins*Publishers* Pty Limited
ACN 009 913 517
A member of the HarperCollins*Publishers* (Australia) Pty Limited Group
http://www.harpercollins.com.au

HarperCollins*Publishers*
25 Ryde Road, Pymble, Sydney, NSW 2073, Australia
31 View Road, Glenfield, Auckland 10, New Zealand
77-85 Fulham Palace Road, London W6 8JB, United Kingdom
Hazelton Lanes, 55 Avenue Road, Suite 2900, Toronto, Ontario M5R 3L2
and 1995 Markham Road, Scarborough, Ontario M1B 5M8, Canada
10 East 53rd Street, New York NY 10032, USA

National Library of Australia Cataloguing-in-Publication data:

Saunders, Charmaine.
Men and stress: the men's guide to positive, healthy living.
ISBN 0 7322 5823 5.
1. Stress (Psychology). 2. Stress (Physiology).
3. Men - Psychology. 4. Men - Health and hygiene. I. Title.
155.9042081

Cover photograph - M. Tcherevkoff/The Image Bank
Author photograph - Dennis Buckley
Printed in Australia by Griffin Press Pty Ltd on 79gsm Bulky Paperback

9 8 7 6 5 4 3 2   98 99 00 01

DEDICATION

I dedicate this book to the men I have known in my life —
lovers, friends, relatives, and to my partner who is teaching
me to trust again.

Most significantly, I thank two human angels, Vivien and
Grant, for coming to my aid in a crisis which threatened the
completion of this book. Without your unselfishness, love,
support and help, I could not have found the peace and
stability to write. Your kindness will never be forgotten.

Last but not least, to my friends who support me from a
distance and leave me alone to complete the writing of each
book — you know I love you even when I have to cloister
myself away, and to my partner who stayed close
throughout, and who helped with editing and suggestions.
Your love is a wonderful gift in my life.

CONTENTS

ACKNOWLEDGMENTS

Thanks go to my publishers, HarperCollins, and especially, my editor, Robin Freeman, who has encouraged me along the lonely way of a writer.

To Cliff Foale, who jumped into the fray when I was desperate and gave me the use of his computer so I could write this book.

Specifically to the following male colleagues who have supported and helped me beyond the call of duty — John McNair, Steve Farey, Miles Glanville.

To Dennis Buckley for his wonderful photo for this book and for always managing to make me look terrific!

Thanks to Grayam Howells who illuminated my way through a very dark time and facilitated life-changing growth for me over the last three years. A lot of your ideas are in this book and I pass them on with love and sincere gratitude.

I also thank the men's group of WA who invited me to speak at one of their meetings and offered me their ideas, insights and input for the book.

INTRODUCTION

It seems appropriate and timely in 1997 to turn my attention to men and their stresses. Over the past ten years, men have often asked me why I haven't written a book for them. Since I have written two books about women's stress and one on teenage stress, it certainly has not been due to a lack of interest in the subject. In my counselling practice, I have seen as many male clients as female, and I find that whilst women are easier to get in through the door, men stay longer in the counselling process. They are more keen to get 'fixed' once and for all, whereas women often see me for one or two sessions and then are anxious to try out my ideas and suggestions by themselves.

I do not aim to set myself up as an expert on men's issues, nor am I speaking for all my gender in this work. Rather, I hope to offer a common-sense look at men in the 1990s, and these are the questions I plan to address:

What are your concerns?

How are things different for you now as compared to a decade ago?

Is the men's movement truly making a difference?

What remains the same?

How can life be a more positive experience for you?

I will share with you the female perspective but I cannot possibly understand how it feels to be a man, to have a man's responses, feelings, needs, psychology. I can only report what my male clients, friends, relatives, students, listeners and readers have kindly shared with me, and I take this opportunity now to thank them for their faith and confidence over fourteen years, professionally, and all my life, personally.

I have been on a spiritual journey myself over the last few years so I have a lot to add to the information in my four previous books. We are, after all, human beings first and men and women second. Therefore much of my experience is also relevant to you. However, as this is a gender-specific book, it must by its very nature be directed to men in particular.

Over the years, I have received wonderful letters from readers in many parts of the world. I hope, fellas, that you will write to me and tell me your stories, and offer your comments on the book. This book is not written with any group of men in mind, but for all who are open to life and to learning. It does not presuppose any level of personal development or education. If it finds its way into your hands to be read, it's for you.

My permanent postal address is Box 637, Subiaco, Western Australia, 6008, my message-taker number is 089 380 4343, my phone counselling number is 1900 229 3523, which can be accessed anywhere in Australia, and my home page address on the Internet is charmaine/koa/com/au.

As with all my work, I plan this book to be joyful as well as informative. I believe in one world and in love and in happiness. Keep an open mind and heart and let us begin on this journey together.

Chapter 1

STRESS-DESCRIPTION AND GENERAL MANAGEMENT

Before we can consider the question of men's stress, we need to have a basic understanding of what stress is, how it affects us and how best to handle it. We have been hearing about stress for several decades, Particularly in the late 1990s. Does this mean that we in the twentieth century have invented this phenomenon? Not at all. Stress is not a modern disease. It has been around for as long as humans have been on the planet, but the condition wasn't given a name until this century. Human beings have been feeling its effects without knowing why.

In modern terminology, the word, 'stress' was originally used in relation to engineering, meaning the pressure on a building in terms of its materials, number of storeys, measurements, and so on. Somehow it was adopted into the vernacular and adapted to human experience. After nearly nine decades of usage, the word suffers from over-use and misuse, so before we do anything else I want to explain how I use the word throughout this book.

COMMON MYTHS

It is important to dispel certain myths relating to stress.

Stress is always bad

Stress is not only necessary for human existence, it can be downright beneficial if harnessed positively. Like cholesterol, we can't exist without it but we don't want too much of it. Without stress, we humans would lack all motivation to get up in the morning and do the things we need and want to do. There'd be no adrenalin rush, no excitement, no passion for life. We'd be positively amoebic!

Stress is the same as tension

For the purposes of clear definition in my previous books, and in my teaching and speaking, I differentiate between stress and tension by calling stress the *external* pressures around us and tension the *internal* pressures within us. We will look at the question of tension in more detail in the chapter on health but, for now, just keep in mind that stress is all around us and impinges on every human being; what we internalise of that stress forms the tension we feel in our bodies and in our minds. This tension varies from person to person, and personality to personality.

Stress is worse nowadays

The world is much more complex today so certainly we would have to concede that life is more 'stressful'. However, the amount of stress that each of us attracts into our daily living has a lot to do with our life style and choices. I like to say that good stress management is really life management. It's all about time distribution, health, balance and self-love, as we will see in following chapters.

HIDDEN DANGERS

If we concede that stress can be positive so long as it isn't allowed to overtake our lives and become excessive, how much is good and how much is too much? I'm afraid, guys, that you are the worst offenders when it comes to saying that you're not stressed, you're just busy! This is one of the most dangerous arguments you can employ because stress, by its very nature, is seductive. It can be very pleasurable to feel all that adrenalin pumping and to fill your plate to overflowing, get heaps done and feel productive and successful. In other words, it's very easy to become addicted to stress, to become a 'stressaholic', and there's no cure! Like an alcoholic, you will have to watch yourself every day to make sure you don't slip back to old habits.

Stress's other hidden danger is its insidious quality. You don't see its harmful effects until it's too late, and sometimes the danger signals are not visible at all until you are seriously into burnout level, and either you drop dead without warning or you become gravely ill. I'm not being in the least melodramatic nor am I exaggerating. That's how stress operates. I was ill for twenty years from stress without realising it. Only when I changed my thinking and my life did I stop being ill, but I remain alert to the old pull of the stressful behaviour.

So many people tell me that the best thing that ever happened to them was the heart attack they suffered or the cancer they developed because it made them look at themselves, re-examine their life styles and make positive changes. My answer is: why wait till you get sick and nearly die to reassess the way you're living and examine the damage to your health, emotional well-being, and relationships?

Stress lowers the efficiency of the immune system and that in turn reduces resistance to infection and disease. Therefore, apart from the daily toll on the body, there's also the very real danger of chronic illness and/or severe sickness if stress is not kept to manageable levels. Some people have a greater tolerance for high stress and some even insist they thrive on it but all of us are affected in an adverse way if we have too much stress for too long. So, the key issues are *amount* and *degree*.

SYMPTOMS

Prevention is always the best way to deal with stress in the everyday sense. Specific stress events can be allowed for and scheduled for, as in the case of moving house or a wedding in the family. But it's the routine stresses that require monitoring and supervision. Bad habits are very easy to form and hard to break; therefore, education of our young people is essential. No matter your age, however, you can break your negative stress habits as I did, and change your life.

Before this can be done, however, you need to identify your particular stress traps, for example, is your main pressure work related? Or is it tied up with self-concept or unsatisfactory relationships? That's a task I would ask you to do right at the start of this book. To help you, here's a run-down of some common stress symptoms.

They can be divided into three broad categories: physical, emotional, mental.

Physical stress

Symptoms of physical stress are:

- chronic fatigue
- chronic insomnia
- headache
- other unexplained aches and pains
- body tension
- listlessness
- inertia
- susceptibility to disease

These symptoms should be checked out medically before association with stress, but if they persist for no biological reason, then the stress factor should be studied in relation to the individual case.

Every stressed client I've ever seen has had trouble sleeping, for instance. One or two broken nights are normal here and there but consistent insomnia is very unhealthy and usually a symptom of stress rather than a problem in itself. (In the chapter on health, I will offer strategies for dealing with insomnia.) The same applies to fatigue. If you've had a long, busy, physically taxing day, feeling tired is normal but if you wake tired every day, even after a reasonable night's sleep, feel tired most of the day and go to sleep tired, you know something's wrong. Stress is very draining, physically and emotionally, so living with stress starts to feel like a daily uphill battle. If life feels like a grind, a joyless struggle, change is imperative and not as complicated as you might imagine.

The location of pain in the body is very revealing. There are certain centres of the body that hold more tension, specifically the head, shoulders, neck, chest, stomach, and lower back. That's why stress often shows up in the form of a headache, and we even have a name for it — the tension headache.

The shoulders and back of the neck physically hold a lot of tension, and when we say someone's a 'pain in the neck' the meaning is more literal than it sounds. Anger, if unexpressed and unresolved, sits in a body site and eventually can show up as pain. It's instinctive to rub the back of the neck and roll the head around when we feel tired, anxious or under pressure.

Chest pain can result from a stress attack or, in severe cases, a 'panic' attack. It feels almost like a heart seizure but is a dull rather than sharp pain, does not have a secondary pain associated with it, and feels more like pressure, a bit like bronchitis or a weight on your chest. It goes away after a few moments but is a very clear warning sign.

Some people take all their anxieties in their 'gut' area and suffer from such conditions as ulcers, indigestion and bowel problems. Around the navel is a very 'psychic' area of the body so anxiety and fear is usually experienced there, while the chest is the heart region and more likely to point up hurts and sadness, literally 'heartache', even from childhood and the past in general.

The lower back represents support; it aches or goes out when we feel overloaded with responsibility or 'unsupported' in our lives.

The body can tell us a lot about our emotional states, as well as the physical, if we are only willing to listen. But remember all these explanations I'm offering are relevant only if you have no known physical cause for these pains and ailments.

Emotional stress

Symptoms of emotional stress are:

- being out of touch with people
- being irritable
- depression
- mood swings
- flare-ups
- feeling isolated and alienated
- loss of libido

When we're overstressed, we tend to withdraw emotionally and have little tolerance of pressure from others. The smallest thing will cause us to flare up or even to cry. After a period of excessive stress, we may sink into the opposite extreme, feeling flat and lethargic. That's just the psyche seeking balance. Depression following stress is normal, and is yet another symptom that requires attention.

A stressed person cannot get along with people in a balanced way that includes a spectrum of emotions. Frustration builds easily and tips over into temper outbursts with very little provocation.

Mental stress

Symptoms of mental stress are:

- inability to concentrate
- memory loss
- confusion
- inefficiency
- disorientation

A client once told me that he realised how stressed he was when he spent an entire day at his office desk just shuffling papers around. He thought he had worked hard all day but in fact he had done nothing constructive at all.

Another example of typically stressed behaviour is that vacant feeling you get when you walk into a room to do or fetch something and then realise you can't remember what it was. Feeling generally confused and disoriented is also a common reaction, as is being forgetful and disorganised. It's very difficult to work efficiently when you're in this frame of mind, and focussing on a task to completion is virtually impossible.

Of course, there are varying degrees of confusion, but when stress overload is at an extreme, even the simplest functions take on mammoth proportions.

GENERAL STRESS MANAGEMENT

Now that you have checked the list of symptoms for evidence of overload, and established what your main stress trap maybe, you're ready to look at managing stress in your life and even learning how to harness it as a positive force.

As we established earlier, stress can be a positive force in our lives as long as we stay in charge and keep the amount comfortable — this is an area that you have to monitor on an individual basis, taking in your needs and your nature. You don't have to limit your activities, choices or life style but you may want to make some practical changes, such as hours of work, or some inclusions, such as a short period of quiet time every day. It may require only an alteration in the way you think about yourself and your life.

Practical strategies

Here are some practical strategies that are simple and yet make a big difference to stress levels:

1 Build in some 'cushions' in your day's activities, for example don't have appointments back to back or overload your day too much.

2 Never eat lunch on the job unless it's specifically a business lunch and even then take your time. Ten minutes here or there won't make much difference to your productivity over all but it can make an enormous difference to your stress levels. If you work at an office, get out for a break during the day, preferably for a full hour. Eat lunch away from your desk but, if this is impossible, take a ten-minute walk outside in the fresh air afterwards.

3 If you're having a particularly busy and pressured day, do a couple of minutes of deep breathing every hour or so just to centre yourself. You'll be amazed at how much easier it is to get through your day and how much less stressed you'll feel at the end of it.

4 Remember that you always have the choice of a negative or positive reaction to a stressful situation, or what I like to call a 'stress event'. A good example is sitting in a traffic jam. Okay, you're running late for an important appointment, it's hot and you're furious. Will the traffic flow faster because you honk the horn, yell out of the window and tap your fingers impatiently on the steering wheel? Of course not, so you may just as well find a more productive way to pass the time:

- turn on the radio and tune into some soothing music
- play a motivational tape that you normally don't have time to listen to
- do some deep breathing exercises
- say some positive affirmations
- do some stretching.

You'll be amazed at how quickly your irritation will pass. You know the saying about accepting the things you cannot change!

5 Find ways to deal with your anger, conflicts and frustrations in a positive way. If you don't, they'll either sit on you and then explode inappropriately; or you'll eventually develop a sickness because of all that repressed negativity. Your stress levels will climb without your realising it till they reach dangerous proportions. (More of this in the chapter on emotions.)

6 Try to have a definite cut-off point each day between work and leisure time. A colleague who had a very responsible and high-pressure job told me that he had a good technique for this. Every day when he came home from work he would take a shower and imagine that his tensions and stresses from the day were going down the plug-hole. This worked for him but you can use any method you find successful. It might be as simple as spending a half-hour in the garden, sitting down quietly when you first stop working, or going for a run. It doesn't matter what it is but if you don't use a mechanical device to divide work from rest, you just never stop. A man I knew developed a heart condition because he used to run in from work, go straight into the laundry, put the washing on, then into the kitchen to start dinner. He was a single father and his argument was that he could keep on top of his chores only if he ran from one to another but he would still have got everything done with a more relaxed attitude. Stress is as much a mind-set as it is a physical reality.

7 Identify your particular stress trap as mentioned earlier and check out practical ways to reduce whatever is causing it, for example a certain person in your life who may be niggling or annoying you. If you can, cancel out all or most of your interaction with them. If this isn't possible, change your attitude to them. This is a surprisingly effective tool. Trick yourself into believing you like them, find some common ground, make conversation instead of avoiding them, and so on. A guy complained to me recently that he has to sit next to a whinger all day at work. He finds it hard to concentrate with this workmate going on non-stop next to him. I suggested that he send the guy good thoughts instead of angry ones because straight away that changes the situation from a negative to a positive one. Next, he could try tuning him out — it's quite easy with practice — and if this still didn't work, to speak assertively, that is, quietly but firmly, and ask the co-worker to please understand that his talking was making concentration difficult.

Use the first rule of positive conflict resolution — state only your feelings about a situation; never go on the attack or criticise the other.

Whatever you decide your stressful habits are, they can be altered or adapted, be they hours of work, type of work, the people you're surrounded by, bad diet, addictions, poor health or sleep patterns.

8 Time management is a key stress reduction tool. Most people get flustered and feel overloaded because they're not using time efficiently. This will be covered in detail in the chapter on work but for now, keep in mind that an ordered work space, short simple lists, clear work methods, well-kept diaries and appointment books and allowing the proper amount of time for each required task are essential for optimum efficiency. Working haphazardly is a sure recipe for stress and poor results.

9 Make lists, plans and goals that are realistic and aid progress. It's always best to organise your tasks in manageable segments rather than plunging in and trying to tackle everything at once. A few minutes every morning planning the day's activities could save hours in the actual process. Have a 'must do' list and a 'wish to' list. It's better to have a list of five items that can't wait and get them done rather than twenty things that you know you'll never get round to. Any extra time you create during the day can be spent on the 'wish to' items. This rule is also applicable to weekly, monthly and even yearly projections. In diaries also, list only definite appointments, meetings and tasks, with a notation for possible additions. If you write twenty things you want to do on a page for any given day and you achieve only twelve of them, you might be tempted to carry the other eight over to the next page. So now you've put yourself under pressure before you've even started the new day. If you continue this practice, you could finish the week with thirty or forty uncompleted tasks — and what about at the end of the month!

Keep it simple, be organised but not to the point of compulsion. Think of your blood pressure!

10 Look after your physical, emotional, intellectual, financial, sexual and spiritual needs on a daily basis. Each of these items will be tackled in the relevant chapters but, on a general note, keep in mind that it's very important to be aware of your mental and physical fitness every day. It's no use trying to make up the sleep you've lost or to counteract all the bad food you've eaten or complaining when you get sick that you should have exercised more. These bad habits have a cumulative effect. Try to incorporate good living habits into your daily regime. I'm not suggesting that you have to be a wowser and not enjoy life. In fact, the very opposite is true. The healthier your body and mind, the more pleasure you can get from just being alive.

Balance is the key word and the cornerstone of all efforts at stress management. Many things will be important to you; therefore, get into the habit of prioritising. Some days work will be given first place in your energies, other days it might be family concerns and at times it's right and necessary to put yourself above all else. By caring for your own needs, you are apt to be less of a burden to others and, indirectly, you will have more to give anyway.

Establish healthy boundaries with the people and demands in your life. Know your own limits and keep to them. Make the necessary adjustments and choices.

11 Give yourself rewards at the end of the day or a specific task. This is not 'skiting' or being vain. It is a sign of a healthy self-esteem and an adult attitude to yourself. Why wait, perhaps in vain, for others to praise you when you can acknowledge your own achievements?

Compete only with yourself. It's fine to want to win but always ensure that you're doing it for the right reasons. Proving yourself to others has limited value; your own opinion is what matters most and when you truly value yourself, you'll find an inner sense of calm that is worth its weight in gold. You'll want to do things well to please yourself.

Rewards can take the form of time off, a sense of satisfaction or a tangible treat such as a drink, an outing, a bath, read, movie — whatever turns you on personally. Some days should be completely given over to indulgence. A guy I knew used to book into a luxury hotel just for one night by himself and drink champagne, watch videos, call up room service, rest, and then return to his stressful media job, saying he felt he'd had three weeks off. Be creative and find ways to pamper yourself. You deserve it!

12 Communication, if effective, can alleviate a lot of stress, both at home and at work. You've heard the saying, 'start as you mean to go on'. Beginnings are very important in setting the tone for future interaction in relationships; for example, a client of mine rented rooms to singles. When he interviewed prospective tenants, he laid out the house 'rules', such as no loud music after a certain time. It might sound controlling but he said it saved him so many hassles further down the track. If a situation is not explained clearly, it's often very difficult to undo the complications once a pattern has been set.

Lack of effective communication is the single greatest cause of breakdown in relationships. Partners are afraid to speak out early in the piece for fear of giving offence but things only get worse if unspoken grievances are allowed to continue. (This skill, as well as assertiveness and setting good limits, will be discussed later in the book.)

13 Specific tools of stress management can be employed, such as meditation, relaxation classes and exercises, Yoga, Tai-Chi, deep breathing. Exercise of any kind is extremely beneficial in reducing stress and tension. Find a form of physical activity you enjoy and practise it as far as possible every day — yes, that includes sex. Sex is wonderful therapy, as is laughing and dancing and singing and swimming and walking and music. The list is endless.

Meditation does not have to be waving in the breeze wearing saffron robes — although that's fine if you want to go all out. You can 'meditate' at your desk or in your armchair or in the garden or in the bath. For me, it simply means slowing down the mind and relaxing the body. Any of these alone won't do; for example men tell me they are relaxing in front of the television in the evenings but I tell

STRESS-DESCRIPTION AND GENERAL MANAGEMENT

them it's no good if their minds are still back in the office or worrying about that sale they didn't make or what they have to do the next day. It's best if you can find ten minutes or more each day that is just for doing nothing. I know this is a foreign concept to us Westerners, whereas the Japanese would think nothing of studying the veins of a single leaf for an entire afternoon. We all need to think less, do less and relax more. Everything will still be done.

KEY STRESS EVENTS

The final area to look at before we leave this chapter is that of key stress events. There are some standard events in human life that are understood to be stressful and can be identified as such. Through decades of research, these have been narrowed down to the following ten:

- Moving house
- Marriage
- A major lottery win or, conversely, bankruptcy
- Change of job
- Loss of job/income
- Death in family
- Relationship break-up
- Major geographical move
- Major illness
- Major accident/injury

None of these is particularly surprising except perhaps numbers 2 and 3, because we tend to think that all stress must be connected to unpleasant things. Yet really joyful occasions can also create stress in the true sense of the word — excitement and adrenalin rush. When they are intensely exciting to the point of altering one's life, for instance getting married or winning a lot of money suddenly, of course the stress would also be matching in intensity.

The bottom line with all of these ten events is *change*. All change is stressful, whether beneficial and desirable or negative and unwanted. Some situations can be planned for, such as weddings and moves, whilst others can't, such as accidents and sudden illness. Experts warn us not to allow more than three of these major stress events in any given twelve-month period as they would constitute in themselves an overload of stress, over and above other factors taking place in a person's life.

The everyday variety of stress problem is of much more concern as it is hidden and therefore much more dangerous.

Various forms of addiction will be discussed in the appropriate chapter, but my final word on the general nature of stress is, if you become hooked on it, as I did, it is as much of an addiction as any other. So beware, and remember, that prevention is far better than cure!

Positive self-talk

- I understand stress to manage it.
- I break my negative stress habits and change my life.
- I identify stress traps and eliminate them, simply by changing my own attitudes.
- I harness stress as a positive force.
- I prioritise to bring balance into my life.
- I always care for my own needs as well as others'.
- I value and reward myself.

Chapter 2

BEING MALE IN THE 1990s

What does it mean to be a male in the last years of the twentieth century? How has life changed for you in the last ten years? The best way to answer these questions is to compare a man of twenty-five today with a man of forty-five. By looking at the differences in their attitudes, life styles and feelings, we will get a clearer picture.

CHANGES AND DIFFERENCES

Attitude

The younger man will have almost totally different attitudes to the older in every aspect of life — work, love, relationships, marriage, life, religion, family. All of these will be examined in turn in later chapters but to encapsulate here, he will be more tolerant, less rigid, less traditional, much freer and much, much more experimental. He will be less ruled by what his parents and grandparents did. For example, a workaholic client of mine told me that he asked his son to work with him on their property one Sunday and his son refused, adding, 'Do you think I want to be stressed-out like you, Dad?'

Life style

Life will be more varied, more interesting, less work-oriented. Younger men expect to spend more time within the family unit these days, and to take more responsibility for domestic activities, some even opting for full-time home duties instead of an outside job. There's a tendency to more movement, from job to job, home to home, even state or country shifts, whilst generally older men will have stayed in their jobs and homes and marriages more as a matter of course.

Feelings

Younger men are more open to their feelings, more prepared to be vulnerable, to admit they're wrong, to show emotion. I had a new client walk in a few months ago and announce to me that he could identify some relationship patterns he wasn't very happy with, that he was aware had come from his family experiences and could he please work with me to clear them! He was twenty-four years old. I have had young men in my classes introduce themselves and then tell a roomful of strangers that they recognise their low self-esteem and that's why they've joined the class. When this first started happening about five years ago, I found it pretty miraculous but I'm glad to say it's a little more commonplace now.

It's already clear that there have been some enormous changes in the last two decades and, as already pointed out, change in itself is stressful. Change has come in the form of internal growth and shifting within the male psyche itself, social consciousness and awareness and, of course, huge differences in the way that men and women interact due to the women's movement over the last three decades. There is now a men's movement and this too has given men permission to look at themselves and their particular issues at a much deeper level.

THE MEN'S MOVEMENT

Naturally I have not attended any male-only meetings or workshops but I have spoken to many men who have run or attended these and I have read the literature. The philosophy is similar to that of Women's Liberation in that it embraces the principles of personal empowerment. Of course, some argue that men don't need a 'movement' because they have never been oppressed in the way that women have. Historically this is true, but, in the present time, I believe men do need to develop their own story, the myth of being male and all that it entails. Men's roles within society have radically changed and if this has not disoriented males as a gender, I'd be very surprised.

Transition

This decade has been one of transition as men come to terms with these changes and how they want to perceive their role in the future. They want the same rights and choices that women have been calling for over the past thirty years.

Transition is always painful as it is invariably a time of confusion. I see all transitional times as analogous to being on a bridge, crossing over literally and metaphorically from one place to another. Instead of a geographical place, it's a psychological place. As you stand on the arch of the bridge, you're about halfway across and you suddenly get the most overpowering urge to run, but there's nowhere to go. You can't go back and you're not quite ready to move the rest of the way forward. It is frustrating and scary and you feel more alone than you ever thought possible. You wish you had never started this journey and had just stayed safe and unevolved. If all this sounds horribly familiar, then you are on your way, but don't expect it to be easy or comfortable. It will be neither. The rewards are long term rather than short so a lot of patience and faith is required.

The other reason for patience is that you can't set the timetable. It takes as long as it takes and it varies from person to person. We live in a time of instant communication, disposable commodities, the 'quick fix' for whatever ails you. That's fine but sometimes, it is only in the middle of our emotional discomfort that we break through: we find answers and receive insights.

Process of change

Beyond personal considerations are the collective ideologies surrounding a raising of consciousness. God knows it takes long enough for long-held beliefs to shift but often, when it happens, it happens very quickly. Five years ago, when I first approached a publisher about writing a book for men, I was told to wait as the men's movement was in its infancy. Presumably, the time is now right. You are ready to read a book written just for you.

Is it safe to assume, then, that the men's movement is thriving? From my research, I'd have to say 'thriving' is overly optimistic, but I think it is gathering force. It has had to be a little radical as all movements do in the beginning, a little 'off the wall'. But the community is accepting that there's a lot more to it than a bunch of guys chanting and beating drums in the woods. If this is a form of protest then it is no more ridiculous than a whole lot of women ripping off their bras and throwing them into a communal bonfire. Men face the fire in their own way — they sit in front of a camp-fire as their forefathers did and chant the ancient songs to feel their primal roots, to get back to basics, to shout their cries of joy and pain into the air and know their souls in the land around them.

Tribal cultures understand these needs but Western 'civilised' Man has lost touch with the elements and nature and spirituality. Somewhere between the boardrooms, the executive offices and corporate building, the simplicity of these longings has become lost in the echoes of time. Men have even forgotten they ever had those feelings. It's different for women who are tied much more to nature by their menstrual cycles, the childbirth process and their conditioning that allows earthiness and bonding and emotion, things lost to men for a long time. Now, men are bonding in groups and talking about their lives the way women have always done. It's different to the 'mateship' they exchange on the sports field or in drinking establishments. This is real and raw and unencumbered by convention or social grace.

By no means are all men ready or willing to participate in this 'new age'. Some are finding empowerment and freedom in other forms, on different paths; some refuse to let the old safe denials go and they continue to hide behind the stereotypical male images. How much longer their peers will allow this who can say. No-one can benefit from any process of change until they themselves choose to embrace it.

The important feature of the men's movement seems to me to be about gathering, about honest sharing and new awareness. How this takes place is far less relevant than the process itself. As always, the public at large hears only about the radical and unusual and we always fear what we don't readily understand. Yet, the men's movement is also taking place in mainstream Australia in ordinary lives and ordinary ways, but effecting change just the same.

Increased understanding

Once, when a relationship broke up, a man was simply expected to get on with it. There were no support groups for him, no network to reach out to. If he couldn't talk to his family or close friends, he was isolated. What if he were left as a single parent by death or desertion or divorce? Who could he turn to? Now, there are countless organisations as well as private groups that help men specifically, especially in areas that were once seen as female territory.

It used to be assumed, wrongly I believe, that men didn't need help or support, but as the world has changed and our gender roles have transformed, men need a road-map to find their way. The best news is that men are finding this situation less and less threatening. They recognise that the society that condemned male vulnerability is now turning on its axis and learning from past mistakes. Of course, we're a long way from full liberation, either for men or for women, and to some extent, those of us on the planet at present are the pathfinders of the future, especially in the realm of relationships. Books like John Gray's *Men are from Mars, Women are from Venus* are pointing the way for more understanding between the sexes.

In the chapter on relationships, we will look closely at the issues of male–female interaction, and how this has altered in the last couple of decades. Suffice it to say for the present that there has been tremendous change, mainly due to the increasing numbers of women entering and staying in the workforce. With women birthing babies and then returning immediately to paid jobs and careers, some men are choosing to stay home to be what is now termed 'house husbands'. If both partners work, men are gradually taking up more of the responsibilities of running the home, income and decisions about finances are shared in an unprecedented way, and women are staying on in their jobs as long as their male counterparts. More couples are choosing not to become parents at all, spawning such common expressions as DINK: 'Dual income, no kids.'

These are just some of the many changes that have occurred over time and are now accepted as the norm. The entire concept of family has altered to the point where it's difficult for sociologists to pin down a standard definition. Single men are rearing children, as are homosexual males and groups of men. Good parenting is regarded as being more significant than gender or sexual factors.

MEN'S STRESS

How does men's stress differ from women's, if it does? I believe it does and I'll try to sum up my thoughts on this without sounding too sexist. Most of it has to do with perceived and prescribed roles. In days past, women were the homemakers and men the hunters and gatherers. There was undoubtedly stress attached to these functions right through the centuries. Then, women got the vote and went out to work and, more and more, have taken their place in society as equals of men.

Women have lost a lot during this process of liberation. As with all revolution has come chaos and change and confusion. Therefore I would contend that the key stress for women in the late part of the twentieth century is the very life style that the women's movement has gained for them. Now, they have the same advantages, same pay, same opportunities as men, and also the same stress, pressure, responsibilities and health problems!

If choices and changes create most of the women's stress, what's it doing to the men? I think male stress is directly related to the social and environmental upheavals that have abounded in recent decades.

The men I talk to are confused about their roles, angry at perceived anomalies, uncertain for the future and resentful about what they too have lost. However, in the past, men's stress came mainly from society's expectations — men must always be strong, men must earn the daily bread, men must support all social systems and take responsibility for all failure, men must make all the decisions, men must not cry or show too much emotion, and so on.

As the decades have moved on, these expectations have decreased as women have assumed more of the power, decision-making and responsible processes, in the boardroom, in the bedroom, in the parliament, in commerce, in fact in all facets of daily life. The younger chaps see this as a relief. They can recognise the benefits of their new choices, of two pay packets, of not having to pay for everything, decide everything, be responsible and support everything. It's the baby boomers amongst you who are floundering because you identified with your roles instead of your true selves. You became your jobs, your duties, your titles, your possessions, your income. You are much more than the sum total of those things and it will only be when you let such outworn concepts go that you will allow women to meet with you, mate with you and interact with you in the way that they've wanted to for generations. Our mothers and grandmothers gave up trying but the women of today refuse to relate in the old way. There is now a potential for intimacy that once was undreamed of. Some older women still find this new concept and practice difficult to adapt to.

All this will be covered in detail in the chapter on relationships but, to sum up here, many of you are still playing out prescribed roles that bring you no joy, living up to every stereotyped rule that you were taught and conditioned to accept. Those of you who are in between, trying to adapt to a new way of being male and yet having all the things you still covet are simply encountering the stress of transition. You are the lucky ones if you've stopped resisting.

The luckiest ones among you are the very young, the new breed of men who are coming out of school, seeing a variety of choices, not just a lifetime dead-end job, procreating and parenting with women who do not expect to be 'kept', pursuing life styles that are tailor-made, not ordained. Look around your streets, shopping centres, suburbs — these men are everywhere. I passed one last week feeding a baby with no woman in sight, just sitting on the ground in the middle of a thoroughfare. It looked the most natural thing in the world but that's a sight we once would never have seen. A male madonna, father and child. Why not?

With all these environmental changes, how can men themselves not change, especially those starting out on their adult lives in this decade? My brief in this book is to look at these outside changes and relate them to males as a gender and as individual men. Chapter by chapter, I will examine each area of change and what it has meant to the male psyche, the stress factor that accompanies it and how to deal with it. Attitudes, values and roles have irretrievably altered, some may say not for the better but all in all, we have made progress as a society.

Positive self-talk

- I am open to change as a liberating force.
- I own my longing to shout with joy, or pain.
- I no longer identify with stereotyped male roles; I am my true self.

Having looked at what it means to be male in the late 1990s, let's turn now to a practical examination of the very important issue of identity. There is no male or female identity except in terms of externalised behaviour and social interaction; all 'true' identity merely entails being human whilst remaining true to one's individual truth. So, how do we access this inner world in a practical way?

GETTING IN TOUCH WITH YOUR TRUE IDENTITY

Each of us has an identity that is made up of pertinent facts about us, the data of our existence. You only have to fill in any standard form these days to know what I mean — name, date of birth, sex, religion, address, phone number, next of kin and so on. This is necessary information for various reasons but certainly contains the most superficial picture of our beings, even on a social level. Our true identities are much more complex and may even be contradictory to our practical details.

From the very moment of our birth, we are covered by known and basic facts. What's the first thing that is noted when we come out of our mothers? Our sex. Then we are weighed and measured and the whole process begins — who are our parents, what hospital we're in, where we live, and later the school we will attend, and so on. All these details identify and place us in our society, and we are hereon judged from them day after day. The list just continues to grow as we get older, and in this era of technology, very little is unknown about us on an official level even by the time we leave school.

If we accept that this is a necessary evil, the price for living in a modern society, the challenge then is to rise above being just a statistic, to hold on to our individual natures, despite the desire of our community to cluster, group and classify us.

How do we do this? By firstly realising that we are more than a collection of physical facts and secondly, to access (a true nineties concept!) our internal identities in a variety of ways. When I first began working in personal development, I devised a checklist to help clients, readers and students work with what I call the 'true' identity. This list of ways to get in touch with who you really are, inside, works very effectively. So I will share it with you here.

IDENTITY STRATEGIES

Using your intuition

The intuition is a very powerful tool. It used to be thought of as exclusively a female province but I see no evidence to support that idea. We are all spiritual beings with a rich inner life that can be accessed with practice. Even without conscious choice, the intuition functions but obviously it is far more effective if harnessed and utilised consciously.

It may be true that women have always felt more attuned to their 'inner voices'. If so, we can once again blame social conditioning as men have always been encouraged to be outgoing, adventurous and focused on action rather than thought or contemplation. We sometimes call the intuition a 'gut feeling' or a hunch. Trust it totally for it is connected to your inner truth and offers irreplaceable knowledge, knowledge that you cannot attain through your intellect. When you are in doubt in decision-making, are faced with a difficult choice or unsure about the truth of a situation, always go within for the answer. It troubles me that so many people still think of this as impractical or 'woolly-headed'. Why not use the tremendous power that exists inside you? You know when someone is faced with a terrible crisis in their lives and they rise to the occasion with courage and strength — do you often wonder where that strength has come from? It rests inside us all the time, dormant like a silent volcano but ever-ready to burst forth into its full potential. Why wait till there's a crisis or special need to tap into this power when it can help you and guide you every day of your life?

I'm often told by students and clients: 'Okay, I'm convinced, but how do I do it?' As with any neglected skill, you have to relearn the steps but if you have the desire, you're more than halfway there.

Meditation is one excellent way to work with your intuition but it is by no means the only way. If you just sit quietly with your thoughts and get into the habit of doing this on a daily basis, you will start to experience spontaneous insights, strong instincts and clear messages from your subconscious. Florence Scovel-Shinn, in her wonderful book, *The game of life*, calls these 'intuitive leads' and she says we should follow them without question because they do not come from our rational minds, or left-brain activity, but directly from our higher intelligence, which knows everything. A psychic friend of mine calls them 'scud missiles' because they just 'attack' without warning. I call them 'zaps' but what name you give them is unimportant as long as you begin to recognise their presence in your life. The more you do, the more you will come to follow them and trust them.

Writing is another effective way to tune into your intuition. Get into the habit of writing down your daily thoughts in a journal. You might be surprised at the things that come out if you allow yourself the freedom to write spontaneously and without restraint. I usually suggest to students that they initially keep a journal for approximately six weeks, just jotting significant events, thoughts, experiences, conversations and so on, as they occur. Slowly a pattern will begin to emerge and you'll see your intuitive processes at work.

Even if you don't want to use your intuition in any sort of formal way, try following the next 'hunch' you get, even if it's something apparently trivial, for example a feeling that you should go into a certain shop. Watch and see what happens. I used to be an academic, left-brain, intellectual, analytical person but over the past eight years or so I have operated more and more from my intuition and now I listen to it all the time.

This subject will come up again and again in the book. I will give you lots more examples of the importance of following your intuition and also illustrations of the frustrations and difficulties that can ensue when you ignore these inner messages.

Your own speech

The things that come out of your mouth are very revealing of your true feelings, especially when you're angry. When we are angry, we have a tendency to say, 'I didn't mean what I said; I was angry.' In fact, the opposite is often true. We blurt out our most heartfelt thoughts and opinions when we are too emotionally heightened to care about holding back. The same applies when we're very upset and of course, when we're drunk. That's one of the reasons people get drunk — it breaks down inhibitions and pretence.

So take note of what you say in these circumstances as you will learn a lot about yourself. I used to say that self-knowledge was at the heart of all personal and spiritual development but I have come to understand in recent years that it is in fact what we *unlearn* about ourselves that teaches us the most. Nevertheless, all around us are opportunities for growth if we only stay alert and keep the right attitude. The key factor is not to be afraid that you will discover things you can't handle. You will undoubtedly meet parts of yourself you won't like but denial is far worse: only acceptance can help us to break through the walls of indifference and negative patterning.

The things other people say

Be they nice or critical, the things others say are again very informative. It's all grist to the mill. Listen, process and then either reject or accept it whole or in part. If someone offers you a critical or even cruel remark, they're giving you a great gift, albeit disguised! You can choose to discard it and regard the person and the comment in a negative light or you can make it serve a positive purpose. Let's say a workmate tells you that you're a bit lazy. Ask yourself if there's any validity to the observation or if it's just coming from a negative place in that person. You might want to think about it for a day or two but don't mull over it for too long or it will just become an anxiety. If you feel there's some basis for the criticism, you can choose to do something about your work performance; if you've affected anyone else with your behaviour, you could apologise, and so on. On the other hand, you might decide that the person who criticised you was just having a bad day and you were the 'bunny', in which case let it go and move on.

Start doing this with everything you hear about yourself, directly or indirectly. Not only will you reduce your stress levels considerably, you will begin to see yourself in a more objective and clearer light that can only enhance your self-image and your dealings with others.

Your reactions and behaviour

Just as you can tune in to your inner voice and the external voices that surround you, you can also start to be aware of the people, things and occurrences that cause specific responses in you, including stress. Remember identifying your stress traps in Chapter 1? Well, this is similar. Take note of the people who irritate you, 'get your back up', the things you hate doing and the events around you that cause you pressure or evoke an emotional response. Your emotions and your physical reactions can provide a huge amount of information.

Have you ever walked into a room and immediately connected with someone standing on the other side? Conversely, have you ever taken an instant dislike to someone you were just introduced to? Logically, it is not possible to like or dislike someone you don't know, so where do these immediate reactions come from? Yes, it's our friend again—intuition. Sometimes it's a warning, as when we say, 'I had a bad vibe about that person.' At other times it's what

I call a 'flashback emotion', literally a feeling that takes us back to another time and place, but is totally real in the moment. An instant dislike could relate to someone this person reminds you of, a nasty babysitter or childhood neighbour. An instant attraction usually spells trouble as we will see in the chapter about psychology.

Certainly take notice of these immediate feelings but be careful — they may not be related to reality so don't take them as absolute truth. Just be aware and learn what you can from them.

Your dreams

I will be looking at the subject of dreams in detail later in the book but I mention here that they are a rich source of intuitive information because they are direct messages from your subconscious. Whatever you're dealing with (or not dealing with!) in your waking life appears in your dreams. Unfortunately, dream language is metaphorical and obscure and therefore inaccessible to the average person. Even dream analysts and therapists can't be absolutely sure of the meaning of any particular dream. Sometimes, the message is sharp and clear; more often, it is heavily disguised in fantastic episodes involving flying or terrifying scenes or confusing images.

It is worthwhile to note and study your dream symbols as, with practice, you will understand more and more about the workings of your inner life from your sleeptime experiences, whether pleasurable or uncomfortable.

Others' reactions to you

Over and above what others say to you, you can also pick up their feelings about you from the vibes you get when you are around them, their manner towards you and the way you feel when you are with them. We say some people, 'rub us up the wrong way,' some drain us of energy, yet others 'push our buttons.' There's a reason for all of these reactions and not all of it is personal. Therefore, if you feel someone dislikes you and you don't believe you've done anything to warrant that feeling, take it with a pinch of salt. Perhaps you just remind them of their third grade teacher!

None of us likes to be disliked but emotions are often irrational and cannot be explained in factual terms so accept that you're going to annoy certain people merely by your existence. Don't waste energy trying to figure out why. However, it can be useful in your bank of self-knowledge, for example, if a particular type of person seems to find you irritating, there's often a very good reason for it, as we will see in the chapter on relationships.

Body language

Your body is giving you constant information if you care to tune into it. Non-verbal language accounts for 85 per cent of all human communication so it's obvious that we are giving out a lot more than we ever actually speak. Through our walk, eye contact, tone of voice, carriage and gestures, we are continually conveying messages to everyone around us. As well as that, we are also giving out unconscious signals that others pick up and use to judge and assess us. Even if you're trying very hard to convey a particular impression but your vibration is saying something else, it's primarily the silent message that gets through. This needn't be a frightening thought but it should be sobering. You may very well ask yourself, 'What is my invisible neon sign?'.

You can read everything about a person's true beliefs, thoughts, feelings and, most of all, self-image from their body language, so observe yourself when you're out in public or around a certain person. Are your arms folded in a silent challenge? Are you mirroring the other's actions because you're in tune with them? Are you avoiding eye contact for some reason? And so on. When a client complains to me that no-one approached or spoke to them at a party, I ask about their own demeanour. It's pretty obvious that no-one wants to talk to someone who hangs their head down and is giving out a strong signal that says: 'Don't bother to come over and speak to me — I'm boring.'

You might say, how can I change my vibration if it's unconscious? In other words, I don't know what it is saying. You do know. You know by the reactions you get everywhere you go. Every other person is simply your mirror. If you want someone to smile at you and be pleasant, guess what — you have to do it first. Research consistently shows that we tend to like people who appear to like us. Also, like attracts like just as opposites attract. If you enter a room in an aggressive mood, you will tend to attract the very person in that room who might be giving out that same energy. That's why people spoiling for a fight often find one!

Let me tell you a personal story that illustrates this point exactly. I was in a great hurry, impatient and edgy when I called in at a busy shopping centre to get three or four items quickly. Of course, I managed to attract every slow-moving person in front of me as I rushed from store to store. When I arrived at the bakery counter, a woman had blocked the whole front of the shop with a double babies' pram. I tried to look round the obstacle to see if the buns I wanted were on the counter and I was greeted with a dirty look so I backed off and waited. After the woman had been served, the assistant tried to give her her change but she had her back turned, attending to her babies. The assistant tried for several minutes and finally I said quietly, 'I think the girl is trying to give you your change.' The woman snatched the money and then wheeled off in a huff, muttering to herself but glaring at me, 'Some people are so impatient!' In that whole huge shopping centre I had managed to draw to me a person who was clearly in the same mood as I! It was like looking into a mirror — then I laughed. I stopped rushing around after that.

Tension in the body

I explained in Chapter 1 how tension is the internal feeling of stress and how it can point up areas of emotional strain, especially over time. Some of the work being done in workshops by what are now known as 'body workers' is mind-blowing. I have seen emotional pain leave a woman's body in ripples just like a snake wriggling out from under a carpet. If I ever doubted that emotion is a physical thing, I no longer do after that experience. The event was triggered by a flashback memory, which brought the hurt back fresh and new, and just as sharp. I too have felt waves of remembered hurt rise up from my depths and pour out of me through crying, moaning, wailing and screaming. Mind release is not enough. Buried memories and forgotten pain must also be released through the body as they are carried there whether we know it or not. I used to be a very controlled person who did not like to show my vulnerability or share my tears but it is so liberating to rock and cry without restraint like a child, because it is the child within us we are healing when we let go like that.

There are specific regions of the body that are more prone to feelings of strain as I outlined in the first chapter. You will be aware of your own 'weak' area so allow it to guide you. For example, if you're prone to headaches, start to take note of when you get them. Is it on a certain day of the week? Is it after you've had contact with a particular person? Is it after you've been through a stress event?

Your body's reactions are extremely telling and form a daily fund of important information, even to asking for the food it wants, the rest it needs, the warnings of the abuse that we inflict upon it. In working with all the areas of your true identity, let your instinctive reactions, including physical ones, be your first gauge. Haven't you ever had a craving for a certain food that you might not even normally like, say beetroot or asparagus? What about all those inexplicable 'gut' feelings you get out of the blue?

I was once at a business meeting where I felt physically ill by the end of the three hours. I thought it was due to being in a closed room on a very hot day, but after I left the room I felt immediately better. I knew instinctively it was the vibes I had picked up from the person conducting the meeting. Of course I dismissed this as foolish and proceeded on my way. I accepted a job with that company and endured six of the worst weeks of my life, directly because of my boss, the person who had led the meeting that made me feel 'sick'. It was an intuitive warning I didn't heed and I realised with hindsight that I had put myself through a lesson I already knew! Now, I always listen to these 'whispers' even if they conflict with what my brain tells me: the brain is full of faulty information and is only the *channel* for thought, not the *source*.

This is a common scenario because we all tend to resist the obvious, especially in matters that are beyond our immediate understanding.

Formal techniques

You can choose to use specific techniques for contacting your intuition: Yoga, Tai Chi, breathing exercises, meditation, and so on. These are excellent for those motivated enough and with sufficient time. Reading is also very good because it can trigger spontaneous thoughts and ideas. Writing is especially good if, as said before, you allow your thoughts and words to flow unhindered.

There are journal-writing classes that teach you how to write your personal story. It is different from other forms of writing because you are not trying to achieve any particular message or aim. It could be called 'free' writing as it comes out of the unconscious part of you and is right-brain activity. If you are a right-handed person, try writing with your left hand. That brings us into contact with right-brain thought and image, quite different from the left side of the brain, which deals in rational analysis and black-and-white thinking. The right side of the brain works with creativity, dreams and imagery.

All these activities simply require desire and practice. At first, it may seem awkward and self-conscious, but more and more, doing it will feel easy and relaxed, effortless. As with every other type of skill, life-skills require practice and patience. You wouldn't just wake up one morning and expect to be able to play a musical instrument you've never learnt. Give yourself the same understanding and patience when learning positive thinking or stress management or better communication, especially when you have to undo entrenched habits.

Positive self-talk

- I am more than just a statistic.
- I refuse to be classified.
- I own, trust and use my intuition.
- I listen to what I say.
- I put to positive use what other people say.
- I am aware of body language — my own and others'.
- I allow the child in me to heal.

Chapter 3

MALE PSYCHOLOGY

My discussion of male psychology is at best academic, but I hope it is also real because I base my understanding of it on the case studies, stories and confidences of my clients over thirteen years of counselling and my observations of the men around me throughout my whole life. My observations must be imperfect, tinged as they are with biases and coloured by my own psychology, but the recounting of my professional assessment will be much closer to the mark as I am removed from the process and in the counselling room no-one lies, except to themselves. An experienced therapist can always sift the truth from the bravado, the denial and the cover-up. I believe, then, I can safely say this is an accurate picture of the male psyche.

Firstly, I must stress that male psychology cannot be removed from human psychology. It might even be argued that any departure results from purely learned behaviour, that we come out of our mothers exactly the same as each other but then are taught to be either male or female. I'm not arguing the nature/nurture debate here but undoubtedly what we learn in the first three years of life is immeasurably significant in shaping who we become, what we think and feel, and how we live the rest of our lives.

EARLY CHILDHOOD INFLUENCES

Each one of us is born with the potential to be naturally joyful and happy. By the time we have reached our third birthday, we are no longer this way. Why? To put it simply — because those who have charge of us play such a significant role. Whoever they are, Mum and Dad, or Mum and Grandma, or Dad and an aunt, or two aunties, or two gay men, they are the gods in our miniature world and we trust them utterly. We learn very early in life to operate around the moods and feelings of others. A baby is totally happy in its existence, just being, but its father may come home drunk every night and slap it for no reason. The child does not understand that its father is in the wrong and it thinks it must deserve this treatment, so very early in life it begins to accept shame and guilt and to take on the responsibilities of others. It decides that it must keep its caretakers happy in order to be allowed its own happiness, so now we see the beginnings of co-dependence. Out the window goes spontaneity, affectionate behaviour and natural exuberance.

I adored my uncles when I was growing up and loved throwing myself into their arms as soon as they arrived home from work, but I soon learnt they were not always receptive to this, so gradually I grew more cautious, watching out for signs of bad moods or tired expressions before I ran for my hug. My natural desire to show affection was already being stifled and by the time I went to school, I had become introverted, fearful and repressed. I only came out of myself when I was in my late teens and then I was told by well-meaning friends that I shouldn't be too effusive as people don't like it!

Within the bounds of good taste, we should do what feels comfortable for us. If we cross over someone else's boundary or invade their personal space, it is their responsibility to stop us. Second-guessing ourselves leads to a fear of taking any risks at all and eventually leading lives of pretence and quiet desperation. It is only our fear of rejection that stops us expressing our feelings, just as I didn't want to be pushed away or growled at by my uncles. That's okay for a child but as the Bible says, let us 'put away childish things' when we grow up. Our only adult fear should be that of deceiving and denying ourselves.

Learned patterns of thinking and behaviour

We bring from childhood everything we see, observe and feel, what is done to us, what is said, and what is not said. Children are watchers, continually mimicking the actions and words of the adults around them. A community service TV advertisment a while ago showed a boy and a girl playing house, acting out the roles they've observed their parents playing. The girl is preparing dinner, the boy walks in and she tells him to sit down as his food is ready. He goes to the fridge and brings out a 'can of beer,' with the words, 'I'll just knock this off first.' The voice over says, 'Every move you make, every word you say, they'll be watching you.' It was, as intended, a chilling message.

If you try to remember your own childhood, you will start to see the early patterns of your thinking emerging. These form the basis of your adult life. What we forget is that a large part of our experience is subconscious, which means that our feelings and choices, though appearing rational, are in fact coming from the past. The reflex emotion we spoke of earlier is a clear indication of this.

A client of mine who was given no birthday attention as a child understandably grew up to be rather negative on this subject. He had low expectations for this day each year but the small boy inside him longed for someone to break the pattern and give him the birthday he had craved in childhood. One year, his partner handed him a birthday gift wrapped in Christmas paper and his first reaction was that he was being given a recycled present, and that his lover hadn't even bothered to rewrap it! Even to a grown man in his thirties, this brought back fresh and new the hurt of a dozen disappointed birthdays — he had to leave the room to hide his tears. His girlfriend realised he was upset, and explained that it was all a joke and his real present was in the next room.

The main point of this story is that we never forget. All these hurts, disappointments, put-downs, neglects, and so on are stored up in the subconscious mind and must be brought out into the light of day if we are to be truly free of the past. Some people spend their whole lives regretting the past, hating their parents/carers and blaming their childhood for all their present frustrations, failures and hang-ups. This futile exercise results in more negativity instead of improving matters.

In the name of love

Psychologists are often accused of attributing all their clients' problems to parents. Unfortunately, the family of origin is where all the first key influences take place —this is irrefutable. Whether happy or horrible, our childhood memories shape us. Laurence Olivier said, 'Behind every front door is a slaughterhouse' — strong words but consider the fact that at home the ugliest sides of human nature are exposed. Members of families, young and old, are ravaged, savaged and torn apart by words, neglect, pain, abuse, violence, alcohol, even hatred, often in the name of love. I'm not suggesting there are no families where people are loved and supported, praised and encouraged; in fact, more and more education means we as a society now understand far more about the importance of positive nurturing. Therapists like John Bradshaw are helping us to see that, to a child, love and attention are just as vital as food and shelter, that denying these things to children is abuse — as much as hitting or yelling. Physical abuse is clear and defined; emotional abuse is much more complex and subtle but no less damaging.

This is not about blaming parents. To the contrary, forgiveness is an essential part of healing and moving on. Louise Hay says, 'We are all victims of victims.' I would say: we are all imperfect beings. Whatever our parents did to us or didn't do for us, they did their best. If they were violent, they were probably beaten themselves as children; perhaps they were under tremendous pressure to take on responsibilities they were ill-equipped for. A friend of mine always says, 'No child comes with a book of instructions.'

It is easy to look back at our emotionally impoverished backgrounds and criticise but judging others always rebounds. I used to be a perfectionist and consequently very hard on myself and everyone around me. I couldn't see that I was spending my life looking for faults everywhere and making myself miserable. We should have opinions and standards but working and living to the best of our abilities is enough as long as we are always true to ourselves. Life *was* meant to be easy. We are the ones who make it more difficult than it needs to be.

MOTHER AND SON

Having established how important childhood influences are, I must spend some time now on the single most influential relationship we will ever have — one with the mother.

The mother–son relationship is generally a very good one. Mothers and daughters have a more complex and emotional link, whereas on the whole mothers are more indulgent and approving of their sons. Usually, men complain to me that it was the father who gave them a hard time, riding them, criticising, pressuring, and neglecting them or whatever. The mother often end up playing the go-between and, in cases of abuse, the referee. Men complain that the mother is molly-coddling the boy(s) and mothers generally say fathers are too hard. Is it because we expect our same-sex children to be us all over again? Are fathers disappointed if sons don't wish to follow in the same trade or profession or are not good at the same things? Obviously, an abusive or over-critical father can leave permanent emotional scars on a boy. That's not to be underestimated, but a cold punishing mother creates a personality that will develop severe emotional problems.

The aloof mother

We've established that children seek approval, that they blame themselves and model themselves on their parents.

So, if the person from whom we most crave love appears aloof, distant, even uninterested, what is the message most likely to be absorbed? That we are unloveable — not unloved or loved insufficiently — unloveable. The core belief most of us bring from childhood is: — I'm not good enough. (We'll come back to core beliefs and how we form them.) Every action, thought and feeling of childhood contributes. You might feel that as a child you adored your mother or that you in fact, hated her. It's all the same — it's love. You craved the reciprocation of this feeling, you did everything to please her, you longed for her praise. If all you got was criticism or, worse still, neglect, you had certain choices — go more and more into your shell, as I did, or become a rebel, because getting into trouble is preferable to not being noticed. By the time you got to your teens and began to see your parents as real people and not as gods, you had lost faith and your illusions and had convinced yourself you didn't care any more anyway. That is how most of us enter young adulthood. It may sound grim but I think it's a fairly accurate picture.

Parents often complain to me that their teenagers seem to suddenly drift away and become monstrous strangers overnight. Apart from the normal teenage rebellion, a shift in the power base is also occurring. The only power teenagers have is to torment their parents and they do this by breaking the rules, being totally unpredictable and pushing their boundaries to the limit. Teenage boys usually start a bit later, about sixteen or seventeen. From this age, you guys are never as close to your families again. You either leave home altogether and contact becomes a once-a-year card or note, or from time to time you make duty visits, that are perfunctory and totally plastic. No-one says anything honest or real. Either you hide behind humour, the good old

Australian cure-all, or you're so polite, you're totally walled off from any real feelings. It can be argued that parents only get the relationship with their children that they deserve. Cold and neglectful parents reap cold and neglectful adult children. Children do not owe their parents love just because of biological connection; it has to be earned. Parents, on the other hand, owe their children everything because they brought them into the world.

The doting mother

Now let's take the case of the, doting, dominating, possessive type of mother. Studies show that background profiles of many gay men indicate the presence of this kind of mother-figure. It's a classic co-dependent relationship, based on mutual need that can be very unhealthy, depending on the degree of closeness. A mother who makes her son feel that he is nothing without her, that she is the only woman who will ever truly understand him, that she loves him most, and so on, is not actually being a loving parent at all, but rather fulfilling her own needs at the expense of her child. I remember seeing a John Bradshaw video in which he was talking about various styles of parenting. He gave the example of the seven-year-old boy who was picked up from school each day by his mother and grilled for ten minutes about how much he had missed her, whether he loved her, how often he thought about her, and so on. The pressure on a child of that age to provide his mother's needs in this way is immense; the mother's behaviour is selfish love at best.

Such mothers are living out their lives through their children, which is unhealthy for both parent and child. One can understand how a male child might be put off women for life by this type of interaction. Fathers in these cases usually stand by feeling helpless: a dominant mother is very often also a dominant wife. After a number of attempts to change this behaviour pattern, they usually just give up. These strong females are not the shrewish, bad-tempered kind (although they can be) but very often are quiet determined women who are fiercely protective and single-minded about their sons.

Apart from any other considerations, boys who grow up in this environment have an unrealistic view of the world and their place in it. If women don't teach their sons, for instance, to share in household chores or play equal roles within the family, they will expect preferential treatment in the outside world, thus creating conflict in their adult relationships. If mothers make excuses for their sons' errors, never ask them to be accountable, spoil them with unearned praise and generally cocoon them from life's lessons, they are failing in their job to prepare them for future life. It's just as harmful as being too much the other way and guarantees that their sons will remain tied to the apron strings.

Healthy love never holds on too tightly, but lets go when necessary. I know many cases where grown men feel compelled to visit their mothers on a daily basis even if married with families of their own, and men well into their forties and fifties who do not yet feel ready to leave home and make their own way.

More will be said on this subject in the chapter on relationships but we cannot hope to understand our psychology without examining our past influences.

How do we escape from the negative aspects of these influences? By forgiving unconditionally, by honestly appraising our relationships with those closest to us, changing the ones that are not working in the way we would wish, and most of all by acceptance of ourselves and others.

CORE BELIEFS

What are core beliefs? They are the beliefs we have deep, deep within us about everything that is around us — ourselves, relationships, home, family, marriage, money, work, country, religion, sport and so on. You have a belief about each thing. It is more than an opinion, which can be changed. Core beliefs are deeply embedded and rooted in our subconscious minds. Therefore they are hard to shift. I mentioned earlier that the core belief most of us carry around about ourselves is that of not being good enough. That is gained from being called 'stupid' repeatedly in childhood, or not ever being given praise or having parents who didn't spend much time with us. These are just examples — it's a conglomeration of every childhood experience.

What sort of life do you think a man is likely to have if he believes deep down that he isn't 'good enough'? Is he likely to be creative and balanced and joyful or would he tend towards self-sabotage and insecurity and unhappiness? He can either spend his life living up to the negative labels of his childhood or he might push himself every single day to prove that he's not the loser he was labelled and felt himself to be as he was growing-up.

Labels

Here's an interesting exercise to try: write down three labels that you have worn and next to each one, write down how you got it, for example 'untidy', because as a child you always had your room in a mess. When you look at all three, you will begin to see the origins of your belief systems starting to emerge. You can then choose to reject these ideas about yourself if you feel they're outmoded.

Even if they're still relevant, try not to use black and white labels about yourself because inside each of us is an unlimited array of polarities. For instance, even if you believe you are still 'untidy', there is a tidy part of you that hasn't emerged or has perhaps been suppressed. We choose on a moment-to moment basis to show certain aspects of ourselves whilst hiding others. We then forget that the other polarity exists and we behave as if it doesn't.

If you put on or accept a label for yourself, you are in effect saying that you are that characteristic one hundred per cent of the time, when in reality you are merely choosing to show that part of yourself and not another. For every untidy part of you, there's a tidy part screaming to get out, but if you don't recognise this, you will continue to promote only one extreme. Most of us are operating on this basis a lot of the time and it becomes very clear when you look at our behaviour within relationships. Long-term couples often display sharply contrasting personality patterns: one partner talks non-stop and the other says not a word; one is fanatically tidy in the house and the other's a slob. Very seldom are they both somewhere in the middle.

Keep in mind that all labels are an attempt to stereotype you and box you into a description that others find comfortable. We all tend to pigeon-hole others and describe them in highly generalised terms, such as 'middle-class', 'executive' or 'blue-collar'. It helps us to understand what we're dealing with, but unfortunately we forget that these phrases tell a very small part of the story.

Voices of the past

Let's take the common example of being called 'stupid'. A guy can grow up and live a 'stupid' life as a self-fulfilling prophecy. This might entail making bad grades in school, dropping out, being unemployed or unable to hold down jobs, getting low pay, engaging in poor relationships, losing money, and so on. On the other hand, he can relentlessly drive himself in his work or business, daily proving himself, never satisfied, a stressed-out workaholic, a walking heart attack candidate, classis A-type personality, over-achiever.

Do you identify with either of these models? I'd be surprised if you didn't because it's at one of these two extremes that most of us are operating. A psychologically healthy person is able to walk between the two polarities, comfortable with his own identity and choices, refusing to wear obsolete labels. When we engage in what is known as 'negative self-talk' we are simply echoing the voices of the past that told us we were 'clumsy' or 'stupid' or 'ugly'. That's why parents have to be so careful in what they say to their children; even nicknames can stay with a child and scar permanently.

Whether intentional or not, parents have the power to do irreparable damage through their carelessness or thoughtlessness. And children never forget. I asked a client of mine, a very successful business man in his fifties, what his childhood label was. He said the Greek word for 'donkey'. I asked him the key characteristic of a donkey and he answered — stupid. On saying this, his eyes filled with tears. In an instant he was transported back to childhood and he was a little boy again, cowering from his father's anger and the label of 'stupid'.

Some of you reading this may be still too far in denial to accept these truths about your own lives. That's okay — I ask not that you take my word for anything, but think about it and test these ideas for yourself. Do you want to be enslaved by your past experience and doomed to relive the same patterns over and over? Studying your patterns is the key to understanding your behaviour in the present, your feelings, choices and thoughts. The patterns are formed by your core beliefs.

Let's say you watched your parents interacting when you were growing up and your observations led you to the conclusion that marriage is a trap. That's your core belief about marriage. You saw Dad trapped by his obligations to the family and Mum tied to the kitchen sink, her personal dreams ebbing away one by one. You might imagine that, armed with that vision, you would go out and seek a partner who will give you a very open and free relationship. Wrong! You cannot reliquish a conflict from the past unless you face it full-frontal! So, you are much more likely to be attracted to a woman who will give you exactly the same sort of marriage your parents had. (We will look at this concept in detail when we consider the laws of attraction in the chapter on relationships.)

You might, on the other hand, become 'commitment-phobic' which is a fancy new way of saying you will always stay one step ahead of the preacher and the wedding-march. You won't know why but you'll keep finding reasons to avoid getting married or perhaps even having long-term relationships. Your logical mind will provide you with lots of plausible rationalisations that you will believe and the pattern continues.

To break out of this cycle, you must first emerge from the fog of denial. Denial keeps you in the past, in ignorance and in negativity.

Accept your dark side

Control is the tool for staying in denial and on the whole I'd have to say men are better at it than women—men are conditioned to do the whole macho, Yang bit. As long as you accept the restrictions placed on you by social stereotyping, you can pretend that you are fine, that you are free of your past, that you are in control of everything. But where is the magic in a life lived without surprise, where everything is planned down to the last detail and spontaneity and joy are strangers?

Once you have pushed past the limitations of a life spent in avoidance of the unpleasant truths of your life, you are free to become whatever you want to be and what you already are. Isn't that the most exciting feeling you could imagine? It's the greatest rush you could ever experience and it will replace all your negative remedies such as caffeine and alcohol and nicotine. It's just life — but lived to the full with adventure and enthusiasm every day. If this sounds like a fairy tale, in other words, impossible, it won't by the end of this book.

Acceptance is the key to everything. You are made up of a mass of polarities. Once you accept this, you will begin to feel much more comfortable inside your own skin. In place of limitations and labels will be freedom and exploration. We each have a dark side and a positive side. It's very important to acknowledge both, and to accept both as equally desirable. As children, only our 'good' sides are encouraged so we soon learn to disguise the 'bad' side in order to avoid censure.

In extreme cases, this fosters the psychopathic mind created by the repression of all the natural darkness that lives within the human psyche. A balanced person loves all parts of himself and knows that if he allows a natural interaction to dance between his polarities, he need not fear extreme behaviour. A repressed person on the other hand, is exactly the type who has to drink in order to bring out his true nature, for example men who can show tenderness and express feelings only when they're inebriated.

The dark side, known as the negative ego, wants to keep us in limitation, in negativity, self-hatred, in pain, in anxiety. It's the little voice that whispers doubts, holds us back, keeps us angry. When you want to take a chance and go for a dream, it tells you you're mad to believe in yourself, that you're heading for a fall, and it recalls for you all the defeats of your childhood and taunts you with failure.

Ignoring the negative ego is not the answer. Instead, you love and acknowledge it as part of you. Say to it, 'I hear you but you're not holding me back. I can do this.'

AVOIDANCE AND DENIAL

These words will keep coming up through this book so it's helpful to be clear on what each term means. They are both essentially psychological processes of defence, what we call 'defence mechanisms'. The purpose of defence in the psychological sense is to protect the psyche from a range of potential dangers — hurt, embarrassment, betrayal, disappointment, rejection and so on.

Avoidance is the refusal, conscious or unconscious, to face issues, and it causes the individual to actually reject the idea that a problem even exists. Some of my clients tell me they've forgotten their whole childhood! That's not a normal situation. For an adult to forget details like names, places and faces is normal but to obliterate the memory of years and years suggests that a choice to forget has been made at some stage of childhood.

Others remember the pain of childhood only too clearly but have rationalised away the importance of those experiences either by selective memory or by minimising the significance of past events.

Neither of these strategies is healthy. It's better to remember and forgive than to deny and avoid. As already said, emotional pain does not simply disappear because we wish it away or block it. It simply comes out in a different form, usually not by choice and much more painful. It's like carrying around a sealed jar that you know contains something unpleasant — you refuse to open it for fear of the contents but eventually the pressure of not opening it becomes greater than the fear of what's in the jar. By opening up the lid, you liberate the 'ugliness' and no matter how terrible, it's now gone!! Isn't that preferable to pretending nothing bad ever happened to you?

We all had painful enough childhoods; it's only the degree of pain that varies. We all came from dysfunctional families but they tried their best. There is only a tiny percentage of parents who wilfully hurt their children; most just make honest mistakes. When people tell me they had 'perfect' childhoods, I immediately ask myself what they're covering up. Either extreme view is out of balance. Examine the good and the painful in your past and when you are able to bring an objective eye to it and to own it all without denial or avoidance, you will know you have healed your inner child (more about this in Chapter 9).

PERSONALITY TYPES

There are three basic personality types: compulsive, obsessive and addictive.

Compulsive

Compulsive people like to have their lives ordered in a particular way. They are the list-makers, the 'control freaks' and the tidiness junkies. Of course, there's nothing wrong with being organised and orderly — it's a question of degree. If you are a slave to your lists, diaries, schedules and habits, as many men are, this is another fertile area for stress overload. If you know yourself to be a compulsive person, try to relax your fixed way of doing things, even if it kills you at first. The world won't end if you go to bed without hanging your clothes up or leave the dirty dishes for a day or two. In fact, I often give this exercise to my classes as a good test of compulsiveness: go home and turn all the hangers in your wardrobe the wrong way or mix up your washing when you sort it — deliberately reverse one of your most rigid habits, just to prove you can.

Perfectionism is a classic example of compulsive behaviour. In my own personal development work during the last two years I have come to understand that perfectionism is a form of death — it kills off all new growth. Once something is 'perfect' it has nowhere else to go but down. My therapist asked me what a diamond cutter looks for in order to ascertain the quality of a diamond, whether it is perfect. I didn't know at the time but of course it's the flaws! So, a perfectionist is actually someone who is constantly looking for the flaws in everything. We all know that there are plenty of flaws around and this means we have a constant source of material about which to complain!

Obsessive

Obsessive behaviour is being very focused on thoughts or ideas, regardless of the appropriateness of this response. For example, you get a fixed idea about something and you narrow your sights until it is all you see and you believe it to be reality, whether it is factual or not. What you *believe* to be reality invariably *becomes* your reality so you need to watch the extent of your tunnel vision. If you're not inclined towards obsessive thinking or behaviour yourself, you're sure to know someone who is and you know how hard it is to shift them from their fixed perspective. People 'obsess' about many things, from others' opinions to infatuations to playing too hard.

Addictive

The above behaviours are really still forms of addiction, which is the most common form of negative focus. I believe that we are all prone to at least one of the three types and in many cases, combinations of one or more.

Addiction itself has several components:

- You hand over your power to something or someone outside yourself.
- Your self-esteem is tied in with this person, activity or thing.
- The object of addiction consumes an excessive amount of time and energy.
- Addiction can be to positive things as much as to negative, for example too much praying, love or work can constitute addictive behaviour if overdone.

I'm often asked by clients or radio listeners how they can tell whether they simply like something a lot or are addicted to it. I tell them to apply the above criteria and give this concrete example. If a guy tells me that he likes sex a lot and wants it four or five times a day, I ask: do you feel it has power over you, do you think about sex to the detriment of your work, health and so on, and finally, do you feel better about yourself when you are having sex? Even a yes to one of these questions would tend to suggest sex addiction. A guy once told me he had to give up his job because he thought about sex all the time. A pretty clear-cut case of addiction!

Addiction is also intense, focused behaviour. When we are engaging in addictive behaviour, we feel 'high' and that makes it much more difficult to give up. Workaholism is a common addiction amongst men and we'll look more closely at this in the chapter on work. And let us not forget stressaholism. As with alcohol, the person addicted to work and/or stress is never really cured. The behaviour can be modified and even altered but the desire to indulge is always present.

We also tend to think that addiction is only to 'bad' things like drugs or cigarettes, but any behaviour that is excessive and disempowers us can become addictive. Sex, money, love, work and religion are all positive things in themselves but can fall prey to addictive patterns if taken to extremes. These topics will be covered in the appropriate chapters to follow.

Moderation and balance, boring as these concepts may sound, are the key to reversing addiction. Of course, chemical addiction needs a combination of physical detoxification and therapeutic counselling and usually involves underlying psychological issues. All addictive behaviour needs time and determination to change because the root of much of it lies in low self-esteem and lack of self-love, which we will address in the next chapter.

POSITION IN THE FAMILY

Your position in the family has quite a strong bearing on your adult personality and the way you live your life. Let me give you a basic character profile for each of the three key positions and then I'll explain some common exceptions.

• **eldest child**: bossy, responsible, a leader, a 'control freak,' a 'martyr,' hard-working, usually successful, compulsive, dutiful.

• **second child**: commonly known as the 'sandwich' child, sandwiched between first and third but I prefer to call him the 'shadow' child because he's always in the shadow of his older brother or sister, classically a very difficult personality — insecure, introverted, easily led, rebellious, dreamy, a 'whiner,' defeatist, passive.

• **third child**: least complicated — parents are usually easier on the third child as they are older now, more experienced as parents, mellowed, more relaxed. Often clients who were the first or second complain to me that the third child didn't have to follow the same rules or get the punishment they did — sorry, that's just the way it is. Because of this, third children are generally happier, more relaxed, less complex. Life seems easier for them.

Studies are only made on the first three positions as any subsequent children just become three recurring.

• **only child**: similar to position one in personality except that theirs will be a more solitary nature; a lot more self-reliance in place of leadership, a love of solo pastimes and pursuits, for example in sport, he's likely to be a swimmer or runner; if musical, will play a solo instrument like piano or violin, often regarded as a 'loner.'

• **exceptions**: positions one and two can easily be reversed if the age difference is small and the second child happens to possess a stronger personality by birth. If on the other hand, there is a very large gap between these two, say four or five years, the second child will assume the personality of the first position or even become like an only child because by the time he's born, his older sibling is already almost at school so interaction is limited. Gender can also create exceptions as a female in the first position might defer to a younger brother, especially if she's by nature more quiet and placid.

These descriptions are not hard and fast but I'd be surprised if you didn't relate to them, whatever your position is in the family.

An understanding of position helps to put into perspective your strengths and weaknesses as an adult. As a therapist, I have made some interesting observations over the years, e.g. many of the men who have consulted me for sexual dysfunction problems were the eldest in their families which implies too much control, trying to be perfect. The body will cease to work in one particular area if there is too much of what we call 'anal' behaviour. More of that in Chapter 6.

A HEALTHY MALE PSYCHOLOGY

This book is not intended to be a deep probe into the recesses of your psyche either as an individual or as a man. However, we cannot talk about stress without also examining how you feel about yourself and being male. Is a man born with a different psychology or does he learn to become a man because he's called a 'boy' from birth and is dressed in blue and is given trucks to play with? In other words, is the male identity as much a label as all the other data? Certainly, socialised behaviour is an inescapable legacy of living in a structured society. Men definitely look and act differently from women but I don't think they're as different as is widely believed. If we lived in another culture, perhaps I wouldn't have needed to write a separate book for men. I didn't choose to do this from a sexist perspective but rather from a genuine belief that men and women experience life and stress in different ways.

Childhood issues are much the same but the difference lies in the way that boys and girls are treated, spoken to, touched and regarded. For instance, clients have told me of their sadness when they got to twelve or so and their fathers announced, 'You're too old to be kissed goodnight any more' as though, by some pre-ordained rule, a boy at puberty should suddenly stop needing physical affection! If anything, a teenager needs more love.

Development stages in life come at puberty, teenage, early manhood, mid-life and the mature years. This book is intended as a general look at the male species, so I will not be examining each of these stages in detail but they will be mentioned when relevant to the subject-matter, for example under 'emotions' and 'sexuality'.

Self-image in our society is so often focused on the external appearance and 'persona', which means 'mask'. More and more, men are being allowed to emerge from the stereotypical stance of 'macho male' and, in Australia, the 'ocker bloke'. There's nothing wrong with going to the footy and the pub and being with your mates as long as you don't close your mind to all the other possibilities in life. A well-rounded man these days can, without batting an eyelid, change a baby, have a beer, attend a football match and go to the opera all in the space of a day. You'll find as you read this book further that I believe the enemy of a fulfilling life is limitation. Always stretch your boundaries, or as the famous character Auntie Mame says, 'Open a new window every day.'

Living a full and joyful life is dependent on a healthy self-esteem. It's much easier to follow the crowd. It takes a lot of guts to be the odd man out, the lone voice in the wilderness, especially in any matter of significance.

A healthy psychology is based on self-knowledge and self-acceptance. You have sets of needs that require feeding every day — emotional, physical, financial, social, spiritual and sexual — don't neglect them or defer them, as is a common practice.

Collective male psychology is supposedly about cars, bravado, competitiveness, aggression, sport, prowess, and physical strength — in other words, the characteristics you're meant to identify with. If you agree, you have a choice to continue, or to broaden your horizons by looking at yourself and the rest of your gender differently. Many of you will have already broken out of this mould, finding it too confining. By the end of this book, you will have been given the opportunity to look at being male in a number of different ways and if you decide that the way you've been living is too stressful and detrimental to your health, you can try some of the many suggested strategies for change.

Positive self-talk

- I unconditionally forgive those closest to me, then I move on.
- I honestly appraise my relationships and change those that aren't working for me.
- I accept myself and others.
- I refuse to wear obsolete labels, or to label myself.
- I aim for self-knowledge.

Chapter 4

EMOTIONS

For years I have been teaching about positive and negative emotions and how to cope with each type. Positive emotions are joy, kindness, tranquillity, happiness, peace and optimism. Negative emotions are anger, frustration, envy, guilt, jealousy, fear, anxiety and hatred. However, I have come to understand that these separate categories are artificial divisions because emotion is energy and therefore it just flows without the need for a label or a judgement. Once you come to accept the simple truth of this, you will find your life and, in particular, your relationships changing.

Emotions are neither good nor bad; they simply exist within the human psyche and they will flow through naturally if allowed. If resisted, they will get blocked and can even store in the physical body, as we discussed in Chapter 1. It's natural to want to promote the more pleasant feelings and cancel the more difficult ones but if you can allow all your emotions co-existence and equal value, there's a lot to be learned from each one. In childhood, we quickly learn that certain emotions are considered 'okay' and others are frowned on. This is how repression starts and as we grow older, we become experts at showing only the feelings we think will gain us approval. Taken to extremes, this can breed psychotic behaviour because it divides the psyche and a whole part of the self is blocked off. Unfortunately, negativity doesn't evaporate if unattended. If anything, it grows and festers until a trigger sets it off and it spews out in a much more severe form, such as violence and aggression. If incorporated into daily behaviours and accepted in a balanced way, the dark side and the light can find harmony within each of us.

I propose in this chapter to examine each of the common emotions of our daily lives in turn, beginning with fear because fear is at the root of all 'negative' emotion, as love is the basis of all 'positive'.

FEAR

The letters in the word, 'fear', stand for 'false evidence appearing real'. This tells us that fear is an imaginary concept. Please note that I speak here of psychological fear and not physical or actual. If someone is coming at you with a knife, you'd feel physical and actual fear but psychological fear is mostly self-doubt and comes from feelings of inadequacy and low self-esteem. It is a fantasy and exists only in the mind. Once you face it, it loses all its power. Whatever unpleasant emotion you're grappling with, be it depression, anxiety, or anger, go within to uncover what the fear is that lies underneath the other feelings. It could be fear of loss, loneliness, being unloved or unlovable, rejection, disapproval, whatever. Face it and it will vanish. The only reason these fears have power over us is because we let them. Often, they are so buried that we don't even know they exist till we choose to start looking at them. No matter how harrowing this may be, it is necessary as fear is an extremely crippling and destructive force in our lives. It cancels joy, stops us living out our potential and swallows up our dreams.

Fear is also always about the future. It's what I call the 'what if' syndrome. We fear what might happen. If we can learn to stay in the moment, fear becomes impossible. Imagine the worst case scenario in any situation that concerns you, then release it to the unknown. You will feel the liberation of this new attitude.

DOUBT, WORRY, ANXIETY

These emotional sides are closely aligned with fear and together form the greatest enemy to happiness that we have. If we could totally eradicate doubt, fear and worry from our minds and hearts, we would not have a problem in life. Think about it. Our negative egos are behind those little whispers we hear in our minds that tell us we won't do things, have things or be what we dream. Ignoring this voice is not the answer. You have to just recognise and honour it as part of you but not give it undue power. The positive part of you is just as valid and important. To be a healthy person acknowledge them both, do what you want, believe in it but don't count on it.

That is the difference between desire and control. Wanting something and knowing you can have it is great;

trying to force it to fit your time and your way brings only frustration. If something you want doesn't work out, there's often a good reason for it. Move on to the next thing and don't waste a lot of time and energy on resentment and bitterness. Second-guessing and doubting yourself creates a barrier between you and your goals. What is known as 'negative self-talk' echoes from the past — the angry parent, the critical teacher, the impatient baby-sitter — their words haunt us in the present when similar feelings or associations throw us back. After years of negative thinking, it's difficult to get out of the habit, but here's what you can do.

First of all, be gentle with yourself. Understand that it takes time for old habits to be eradicated. When you find yourself thinking negatively, which could be hundreds of times in a day, gently replace the thought with a positive one. Take self-criticism; if you make a mistake or forget to do something, you might be inclined to call yourself a name (remember childhood labels) like 'stupid' or 'careless'. Just say to yourself — I'm not stupid, I just made a mistake. With time, this will become an automatic response and you will think less negatively overall. It is a form of reprogramming. You're undoing the layers and layers of garbage you've absorbed ever since you were born, because even before you had words you took in feelings and atmospheres.

Secondly, write down a list of common responses and situations that you think you're dealing with negatively on an ongoing basis. Now next to each item write a positive alternative. You might be amazed at how many times you react negatively on any given day but by writing it down you bring awareness to your most vulnerable areas and you can start the process of change.

Lastly, by embracing even the negative parts of yourself, you will differentiate less and less between what you like and what you dislike about yourself, thus accepting yourself in a more whole and loving way. This is the best cure for negativity I know — when you love and accept yourself, you have to feel that way about others. Self-criticism generalises into critical attitudes about life and other people. This will be discussed in fuller detail in Chapter 9. Doubting something or someone you feel uncertainty about is one thing but worrying when you have done your best, or beating yourself up after the fact of an error or misjudgement, suggests lack of self-trust. It's very difficult to trust others when you cannot trust yourself. Often this translates into 'blowhard' behaviour, arrogance and bravado because of the fear of being caught out in a mistake.

Generally, men have more of a problem with this because society places such a lot of pressure on men to be strong and 'perfect'. The desire for perfection leads to problems with control again because there is no such animal as a perfect person and in order to keep up the illusion, we have to be constantly in overdrive. The voice of doubt in psychological terms is the part of you that will hold you back and keep you locked in insecurity by limitation, so watch out for it.

Worry and anxiety differ insofar as worry is concern for a situation or person that actually exists whereas anxiety, like fear, is a creation of the negative mind. Of course, anxiety can actually be a chronic mental condition and comes in various forms, notably obsessive-compulsive disorder and phobias. Phobias are irrational fears of anything from insects to lifts to heights. If sufficiently extreme, they can take over a person's life, for example imagine never being able to ride an escalator or be around a particular colour. Obsessive-compulsive disorder takes the form of an extreme focus on a particular behaviour or habit, usually cleaning or tidying, to which the sufferer is tied without respite.

These anxieties require professional therapy as they are often symptoms of wider psychological problems, for example one client who suffered from compulsive cleaning believed that her home was actually riddled with germs and that if she didn't keep cleaning non-stop, her children would die! Do you see the connection? It wasn't about the act of cleaning but what it represented, in this case her deep-seated fear of life, her insecurities and the desperate need to protect her children taken to a pathological degree. Her belief was not irrational to her but totally real.

The type of anxiety more likely to affect the average man is the everyday variety. We all build up imaginary worries in our minds and they can become so real we believe them absolutely. Some live with chronic anxiety which is mild but nonetheless crippling, for example many men report to me that they either wake up every morning feeling a vague sense of anxiety or they go to sleep anxious at night. In its very nature anxiety is irrational, that is not tied to a reason. It often has its roots in childhood feelings; bedtime anxiety could be attached to fears of bed-wetting or insomnia; waking anxiety could be related to a dislike of school or fear about what the day will bring. This is then carried over into adulthood and can become a recurring pattern even if it is no longer relevant. If we can get to the root of the anxiety, it can be dispelled with time and patience.

There's more choice with worry, which also can be a learned habit. Regardless of the cause, worry simply doesn't help. It in fact creates a new problem so that you finish up with two. I don't think anyone would willingly choose to double their problems in life. Again, awareness can make all the difference. You have the power to stop being a worrier if you wish. It all begins with desire, then you start practising as you would any other skill. I believe that if you can't change something, let it go; if a situation is out of your hands, worrying won't make a jot of difference while positive thinking can. People tell me that they can't help but worry if their children are sick or other loved ones are in danger, or they worry about the state of the world and whether they can pay their bills. How will this help? Your pattern of worrying is a habit that you can break in the same way as you give up smoking or eat better or get more exercise — with difficulty. But persistence will score a victory.

ANGER AND AGGRESSION

Anger is an interesting emotion because, on the surface, it appears to be one of the 'negative' ones but in fact it has great powers of healing and like stress, if handled properly, can actually be an ally.

Anger is one of the most repressed emotions in childhood and therefore one of the 'hidden' problems we carry with us into adult life. You know the old therapist's joke — 'if you're happy, you must be in denial!' I don't entirely agree for reasons that will be made clear in Chapter 9 but certainly a lot of us mask our childhood pain so successfully, especially in our twenties, that we can submerge whole tracts of experiences, usually unpleasant ones. When a client tells me he can't remember his childhood, I know that he has either chosen to forgot or has subconsciously cancelled out his memories. Men often feel that talking about childhood or the past is holding on or blaming their families. As I've already said elsewhere in the book, the opposite is true. By facing the past squarely, you can be free of it forever.

Children have a lot of anger because they live such a powerless existence. Decisions are made around them, rules are often arbitrary, they're forced to suffer injustices and even cruelty in silence. Any show of anger is heavily frowned upon; instead of teaching their offspring how to deal with their anger and frustration parents — especially in previous generations — punish temper tantrums and force children to hide their true feelings. That is precisely how most of us as adults deal with our anger — we cover it over, absorb it into our bodies and then let it out when we can no longer stand the pressure. In fact, the lucky ones let it out, but some hold on to anger for years and years. Can you imagine the harm it does to your body and soul? The next time you observe an old face or body, take note of the evidence of repressed anger — the permanently pouting mouth from all the resentment left unspoken; the deep-etched lines of disappointment and broken dreams; the bent back and twisted limbs of frustration and hatred.

Learn to deal with your anger in the moment so that you don't have to live a life of quiet desperation. So many of our common expressions speak the truth of the human condition, for example 'stewing in our own juices'. Doesn't that conjure up exactly the kind of destructive fermentation process I've been describing?

What to do about it? First of all, make an honest appraisal of the way you currently deal with anger. Are you a stewer or a blower, a sulker or a yeller? Very few of us deal with anger constructively so if you're thinking you don't have a problem with anger, think again. If you're saying to yourself that you never get angry you've got the biggest problem of all. Where do you think all that anger is going? Sure, there are more placid people in the world who don't get roused or upset easily but I'm not talking about yelling at a neighbour or a passing car — I'm talking about deep-seated anger from the past which has never been released. Most of our present-day anger is in fact about history. We are really angry with someone from the past and they're the ones we should be directing our anger to. But often we don't know that or the person has left our lives. When we yell at, frown at, sulk with or reject a person who has not deserved our anger, we are experiencing what is known as 'misdirected' or 'misplaced' anger.

There's a famous cartoon that depicts a man who, having been told off by his boss, goes home and fights with his wife who slaps her child who kicks the dog. The message here is clear — not only do we take out our anger on innocent parties, we go down the hierarchy to where we feel safe to vent our spleens. There are generally two types of people we take out our anger on — the stranger we'll never see again or the closest people to us who will let us get away with it. When we swallow our anger, it can come out in the most unexpected, inappropriate and sometimes destructive way hours, weeks or even years later. To avoid this, we can apply certain rules of anger management which will help.

Managing anger

The key is to learn to release anger in a positive way. Here are some suggestions:

- Having good assertiveness skills helps a lot because you can then speak your truth quietly as things annoy you rather than wait until the pressure builds to an intolerable degree and you have to explode.
- Communication skills in general are important as a lot of stress is created by what is left unsaid. You may think you're being patient and tolerant but if you secretly resent what is being said or done and you keep saying nothing about it, the problem doesn't go away; it's just being buried.

- Find daily outlets for releasing anger positively, for example exercise is excellent for reducing tension; meditation is great to keep you centred and calm no matter what's happening around you; practise the stress management techniques described in Chapter 1.

- Writing is one of the best tools I know for releasing anger. If you have a grievance with someone and, for whatever reason, you can't deal with it directly, write all your anger down, call them everything and anything because you're not going to send the letter anyway. Get into the habit of writing down your feelings, ideas, dreams, fears and so on, on a regular basis. You'll be surprised what you come up with, especially if you let go of control; you'll also release a lot of spontaneous insights this way. A daily journal is a good idea or you can just sit down when you're feeling angry or tense and let the pen flow. This is called inspirational writing and comes from your right-brain centre where all your creativity, imagination and intuition resides. Too often, we ignore this source of wisdom in favour of the more rational, analytical left-brain activity.

- Get to the source of your anger and deal with it. If it's a person, event, past issue, situation, place or whatever, face up to what has upset or is upsetting you and get it out in the open. People often have grievances with parents or teachers from the past and obviously it's not always possible to have it out with a particular person if they're dead, in another location, are too old or refuse to listen. In these cases, writing a letter as suggested is the best solution or if the person in question is dead, you can go to their graveside and actually talk to them. No, this is not silly. You're sure of a captive audience and the emotional liberation of such an action is indescribable. Even talking to a photograph is very effective. Any of these methods will ensure that you are going right to the heart of your deep-seated anger; your anger can be healed and you don't have to dump it any more on the people around you who haven't hurt you. Even if someone you love does hurt you in the present, odds are you're reacting from the past and that's neither fair nor very positive.

So, if you find yourself getting angry, whether the cause is clear or unclear, trivial or significant, stop in your tracks (it's the old 'count to ten' thing) and preferably leave the room, cool down but don't just suppress the feeling of anger as that's a temporary answer — use the anger energy to reach the source, ask yourself what triggered it and try to remember a similar event from the past that might have an associative memory for you. This in itself is healing. You can always go back and deal with the problem in the present but take responsibility for your own anger first.

- If necessary, get right away by yourself. Go into the bush and scream till all your tension is gone, hit or throw something inanimate like a pillow or a piece of hose or a stick. This works particularly if you have pent-up tension that has accumulated over a stressful period or when you first start releasing anger — it's important to let it out in a physical way as explained before. Losing your temper, hitting out, verbal abuse, violence, swearing, aggression constitute poor anger management and usually result from the frustration that comes with overwhelming anger, causing a loss of control. There's necessary control and unhealthy control. Being out of control in one's behaviour, especially if it causes distress or harm to others, is not good but letting go of the reins in order to experience life more fully and spontaneously is very desirable.

A client of mine, a seventeen-year-old boy, had a very severe anger problem. When something triggered his rage, he would black out and be unable to recall his words or actions the next day. It was obvious when I met him that he had some sort of deep-seated anger that needed to see the light of day. We unearthed the trouble: he was the second child in the family, the elder child being another boy. My client felt an overwhelming pressure brought about by feeling inadequate against his brother, unable to compete. Whatever he tried to do, his brother had been there first. To add to the conflict, he loved and admired his brother so, at times, the rage inside him became so overwhelming he just opted out by blacking out. This is an extreme case but we all use anger in many different ways to avoid dealing with our various problems, hurts and conflicts. As I said in the beginning of this section, anger can be a very powerful healing tool if used correctly. Make use of your anger to better understand yourself and your past.

Conflict resolution

Conflict resolution is a valuable tool for dealing with chronic situations or a stalemate between individuals or groups of people. It's not for one-off arguments or an occasional disagreement. It is a very structured process and has distinct steps:

1 Set up a designated time and place to discuss the conflict and the resolution process.

2 Deal with your emotion before you come to the meeting. Conflict resolution cannot take place in an atmosphere of tension or anger.

3 Each person outlines his grievances and side of the argument.

4 The issues are clearly stated as a sum-up of what each party has said.

5 Brainstorm solutions and ideas for compromises to the situation.

6 A plan is put forward that all parties agree to trial.

7 A time frame is agreed to and another meeting is arranged to review the resolution progress, at which time amendments and adjustments may have to be made and another trial period agreed to.

By this system, conflicts can be clarified and dealt with in an unemotional, rational way. Often long-standing disputes continue because each party is too emotionally caught up in one side of the argument and cannot see the wider issues. Of course, the process I've described works only where both parties have an investment in finding an equitable outcome. Very often I am told by clients that their spouses/partners refuse to arbitrate or seek a workable compromise. Naturally they find this situation frustrating and they ask me why. It's easy to understand. If someone has invested in things remaining the same, he or she has no interest in discussing change. As I've mentioned, change can be very fearful, especially if the person hasn't chosen it. The usual reaction is to resist and to attack the other person for trying to improve things. Blaming others creates a smokescreen that prevents us from looking at ourselves.

How do you resolve conflict with someone who refuses to even admit anything's wrong? By all means suggest a resolution process. If one party is resistant, it's often helpful to have a mediator present, an impartial third party who can help to clarify each person's points as they are raised and act as a buffer if contentious issues arise. That's why marriage counselling is so effective, but again, it works only when both parties are interested in conciliation.

If your partner absolutely refuses to participate in any resolution process, you always have the choice of terminating the relationship or you can try changing in yourself whatever bugs you about the other person because remember, we are all mirrors for each other. By changing yourself, quite surprisingly, the other person is forced to change also. The most obvious example of this is in your interaction with that person, your responses and reactions. Let's say your typical response is irritation to silence. Try a different approach and watch the effect. There may be no change the first couple of times but keep it up and gradually, you will notice a difference. One client who was living with an alcoholic decided to learn for himself about addiction. He attended a course without telling his partner and to his great amazement, his partner stopped drinking! I can only attempt to explain it by saying that it has to do with energy. When you're worrying a situation to death, nagging about it, worrying about it, you increase its power so that whatever you perceive as a problem only gets worse. By dropping the ball, so to speak, you release the negative energy and things have a way of correcting themselves. I've seen this happen so many times in my own life and have heard about it from others that I have absolutely no doubt it works. Try it for yourself the next time you feel you've reached a stalemate in a situation — just let it go and forget it. It's no good if you say you'll let it go but then you keep thinking about it. In other words, resolve the issue with yourself, make it right for you and then stand back, or as I like to put it, turn your face away and do something else.

This is particularly effective after relationship break-ups, where one person refuses to participate in closure. In order to move on, the remaining partner has to achieve closure alone, which can be done and I'll tell you how in Chapter 5.

As long as we're alive and human, there will be conflicts of various kinds in our lives but if we have the right attitude to them, they can be learning experiences and opportunities for growth rather than problems. The resolution process is particularly effective in the workplace, neighbour disputes and family conflicts. Keep in mind that overt conflicts can often disguise deeper resentments and issues, particularly in personal disputes. A wife who complains that her husband is always home late for tea may in fact be feeling unloved and lonely but doesn't know how to express it. We should always seek the hidden messages in quarrels and listen to what is blurted out in anger as we saw in Chapter 2.

Conflict is not negative in itself but can become so if we hold onto it for reasons of spite, power or pride. So, look at the conflicts in your life and decide which are worth continuing, which could stand an honest appraisal and which could just as easily be ditched. You might be pleasantly surprised at how unimportant some of the so-called disagreements in your life really are once you let them go. Hanging on is very harmful to your mind, body and spirit, and of course, your stress levels!

GUILT

Guilt is another irrational emotion in that it has little to do with fact or reason. You can feel guilty just waking up in the morning. If you grew up in a family where blame was commonplace and everything that went wrong was somehow your fault, that becomes your expectation in adult life.

It's important to distinguish between guilt and remorse. Remorse is feeling sorry when you've hurt someone or you know you've done wrong. In that case, apologise, make amends and move on. However, because guilt is a vague sense of being 'bad' or unworthy or wrong, it's a lot harder to come to grips with it. People around us stand to gain a lot by promoting our sense of guilt, a trap to watch out for. Parents use emotional blackmail to make children do what they want; children use guilt to get their way with parents. In a thousand ways, we're all doing it to each other every day because guilt is a very effective tool.

It no longer has power over you once you have worked through your past issues and realise that the old belief patterns you brought from childhood are no longer applicable. So if someone criticises you, you can respond as an adult and not as the hurt child you carry inside you. An adult considers the criticism and acts on it or releases it. A child reacts from an emotional place, taking every criticism to heart and responding without thought.

Take responsibility for your actions and behaviours by all means but don't let anyone put *their* issues onto you by trying to make you feel guilty. *You* are the only one responsible for your morals, ethics and values. Live only by them and refuse to explain yourself to those who would demand justification for your decisions and choices.

Guilt is a very destructive emotion and can eat away at your self-esteem if you're not aware of it. Be your own person and recognise guilt for what it is — another echo from the past that would keep you locked in its grip if you let it.

JEALOUSY

Jealousy is a symptom of insecurity. It is never really about what your partner is doing, whether she flirts or plays up or has other men after her. Trust comes from you, not the other person. If you are incapable of trust, look within to find out why. Being suspicious and insecure is learned behaviour and, again, has little to do with the present. If you judge your partner to be an untrustworthy person, why do you stay? If you judge your partner to be a trustworthy person, why do you doubt? Remember what was said earlier in this chapter about doubt and how it can confuse you and erode your happiness. Trust has to be one hundred per cent. If you have to check up on someone or question her integrity, you don't really trust. Lack of trust comes from fear, fear of being let down, of being wrong about someone, of being played for a fool. If another betrays you, surely that person is the fool, not you. Follow your instincts and you'll never be taken in but once you give your trust, give it wholeheartedly, without reserve and without conditions. It's very difficult for most of us to do this because childhood experiences that took away our trust are not easily forgotten. We apply self-protection in adulthood to guard against the same let-downs that hurt us so much, but defence mechanisms also keep out the things we want, such as intimacy, bonding, closeness, sharing and communication.

Most of us feel jealous at times with our loved ones. Perhaps we didn't get the closeness we wanted from our parents when we were growing up or we were never taught to share the people we love. Whatever the reason, a small amount of the green-eyed monster is acceptable. It's only if our jealousy reaches destructive proportions that we have to examine it and do something about reducing it. Many relationships are destroyed by persistent and unreasonable jealousy.

Possessiveness is a little different and again, is okay in small doses. Loving with open arms is frightening for us — what if we lose the one we love? What if we can't get what we need? What if we get hurt? Well, the chances are pretty high that when you love you risk hurt but what's the alternative? Play safe and be half-alive?

Try to love everyone in your life with respect for their individuality and differences, not concentrating on how they can fulfil your needs. You can never own another human being, not even your children—they are merely in your care. In relationships with lovers and friends, sharing should be the keynote, not possession.

LONELINESS AND SHYNESS

Loneliness is not the exclusive province of the shy. Even the most flamboyant personality can feel alone and lonely at times. First of all, I'd like to distinguish between these two states.

Being alone can be joyful, nurturing and totally fulfilling. It's a mistake to endure the times you have alone as if they are undesirable and only acceptable when there's no alternative. You should choose to spend time alone regularly, schedule for it, enjoy it. Out of solitude comes spiritual refreshment and mental relaxation. Learn to enjoy your home and get out in nature, walk and meditate, clear your thoughts.

Loneliness, on the other hand, is a feeling of emptiness, sadness and isolation. We usually feel lonely at times of least connection with others, notably just after a break-up or when we're living alone for the first time in a while. Most people spend their whole lives avoiding this feeling, filling up their hours any way they can to ensure they won't have to feel bored, depressed and unwanted. Of course, anything can be turned around with the right attitude. If there's a specific reason for your loneliness and you can recognise that it's temporary, allow it as a time of healing, which is very necessary.

Managing loneliness

Loneliness can be habit-forming so if you feel you are getting into a rut, accepting your chronic loneliness as inevitable, then you need to change your thinking. Here are some practical suggestions about loneliness that might help you make a new start:

- Loneliness is only 'bad' if you see it that way.
- Don't rely on other people to keep you amused. Develop your own interests.
- Keep in mind that everyone is lonely sometimes, even famous and successful people.
- Keep busy but don't just fill in time — do things you enjoy.
- Don't play-act about your feelings. Deal with people honestly, even if it means putting yourself on the line.
- Reach out to other people; closing in on yourself only increases loneliness.
- Don't waste energy in wishful thinking or envying others. Appearances aren't always real and if you were someone else, you might be a lot worse off. Enjoy being you.
- A bright, happy person is rarely lonely. True isolation comes from self-centredness and lack of concern for others.

- Remember it is possible to be lonely in a crowd. It is only inner strength that prevents loneliness, not riotous company and endless partying.
- Happiness is a condition, not a goal. Inner peace lasts forever.
- It is better to be lonely than to stay in a destructive relationship. Discover all the wonderful things the world has to offer if you're alone for a time — art, literature, nature, animals, children, culture, sport, movies. Lots of things can be enjoyed alone.
- Allow yourself to be depressed or discouraged sometimes. It's good for the soul. It's all part of the human condition and more honest than putting on a happy act all the time. True friends will accept you, moods and all.

I believe we are most lonely when we feel discouraged by our efforts to create a happy life for ourselves, when we're missing a particular person, place or situation, when we are alone by circumstance rather than choice. Remember you are never stuck; you always have choices.

Instead of sitting by yourself in a lonely room, phone someone who may be feeling the same and take a risk. Get out into the swim of things even if it's scary. You'll never know till you try. This theme will be picked up in the next chapter but let me tell you a brief story that illustrates the point I'm making.

A single client of mine took himself off to a well-known pub for meeting women. He sat in the corner for over an hour, watching the proceedings, feeling a bit uncomfortable and wondering why he'd bothered to come. As he was about to give up and leave, he saw a woman friend and she brought a couple of others over to his table. One particular woman struck up a conversation with him and the next thing he knew, she'd asked him out. This is a guy in his sixties so you can imagine his surprise. We're living in the nineties — anything goes!

DEPRESSION

Depression is at the other end of the scale to stress as it is a low state of being while stress is a heightened consciousness and brings on a 'high'.

The word 'depression' says it all — the sufferer feels pressed down, blue, 'low'. Again, this condition can constitute a mental illness and is not to be taken lightly if chronic. However, most of us experience mild or severe depression as a periodic condition and it goes away by itself within a few days at most. The best way to deal with it is to let it take its natural course. By judging and analysing it you can actually prolong it.

Interestingly, depression often follows a period of stress and there's a definite link between the two even though they're opposites. It's as if the psyche seeks to balance itself so just allow it and it will soon pass. Depression is not a particularly pleasant emotion so we tend to want to make it go away very quickly, especially if we are with a depressed person. The worst thing you can do is tell a depressed person to 'snap out of it' because one of the key symptoms is inertia—lethargy—which means the inability to mobilise oneself. If you can bring yourself to do one small action such as walk round the block or make a cup of coffee, it'll start to break the depression's grip but it will take time and patience.

If you feel your depression is overtaking your life or preventing you from functioning normally, you may have to go through short-term drug therapy or psychiatric treatment.

But if you just wake up some days feeling 'down', it's perfectly natural. Accept it as I have suggested you do with all your emotions and go on with your day as best you can.

A young client of mine couldn't understand why he was depressed a lot of the time. He had a good job, a girlfriend, a nice flat but all he wanted to do was sit in his lounge in the evenings and feel depressed. I suggested that rather than feel bad about it, he say out loud, 'Here I am, sitting with my depression and it's okay.' After a while, the fact of being depressed had little effect on him and he gradually stopped feeling it altogether. It really works. If I were to suggest to you that you should sit in a room and allow yourself to feel as depressed and miserable as you possibly can for half an hour, you'd never last out the time. It's almost as if by getting permission to do it, all desire for it is lost. It's important to note here that a lot of our so-called negative feelings grow because we are told not to feel them. Guilt is a great promoter of negativity.

SELF-ESTEEM, SELF-LOVE

So far I have spoken mainly about the 'negative' emotions, because they tend to control our lives a lot more than the positive ones. I want to speak about love in the chapters on relationships and positive thinking but now, I want to discuss self-love, which is linked to issues of identity and psychology.

Without true self-love none of the strategies I am recommending in this book will work for you, for the simple reason that self-love is the basis of all of them. You cannot be a good communicator, a positive thinker, a happy relater, an unstressed person or a balanced human being without being able to value, accept and trust yourself. Let me talk for a moment about polarities.

Polarities

Polarities are the opposing characteristics that exist in each of us. None of us is all tidy or diligent or rude or noisy. For each one of these traits, we also possess the opposite number. Thus, you are equally tidy and a slob; diligent and lazy; rude and polite; noisy and quiet. The only difference is what you choose to show in your persona (outward mask). As a child, you made some conscious and subconscious choices to display certain behaviours that, for various reasons, suited your purpose. For example you might have been part of a very noisy family and found that you got more attention by being the only quiet one, or you were naughty and rebellious because that's the only time your father spoke to you. Children would rather get negative attention than none at all.

Once you accept that, you will stop labelling yourself in one-dimensional terms and start to experience life more fully because you are not restricting yourself continually. You see, many of us are scared to experiment with ourselves. And have you noticed that others prefer to pigeon-hole you as well? Those close to you have an investment in your being a certain way. Any deviation from that, no matter how minor, causes them to feel insecure. Usually I warn my clients, when they start making personal changes, to expect flak, criticism and resistance from those around them. That's why you have to be really motivated if you want to change aspects of yourself — on the whole, you won't get positive reinforcement.

As soon as you begin to accept polarities in yourself, you stop judging others' behaviour, especially when you remember that the very things that irk you about others are often the traits you dislike in yourself. Practise with the parts of yourself you're less familiar with. Be less rigid in your thinking. Free your mind and you free your life. And the next time someone is really bugging you, especially a stranger, ask yourself what you see of yourself in that person's behaviour. Then say out loud or in your mind, 'I love the . . . . in me that I see in . . . . ' Sample: 'I love the miser in me that I see in Fred.' Perhaps you've always fancied yourself to be very generous, well, allow yourself to accept that a part of you is just as tight as your friend, Fred and Fred's behaviour will stop irking you.

Follow your instincts and you can't go wrong. Listen to others but hold your own truth even if everyone else opposes you. When you can live with that kind of courage and trust, you will begin to value yourself in a way that you can't presently imagine. It will no longer matter what you were told in childhood or what happened to you in the past. You will learn that invaluable lesson called 'living in the present', which is hard at first but once conquered becomes second nature. You may think you have good self-esteem now because you have a nice home, money in the bank and a status job, but these things are only the trappings of your life, the false securities you have used to shore up your fears and feelings of inadequacy. Imagine yourself without all your symbols of wealth and success, then see if you still accept yourself. When you love yourself in a real way, it's not conceit or arrogance, and it's not plastic or superficial. It's deep and it's forever. Nothing and no-one can take it away from you.

Wouldn't you like to have that kind of security instead of the kind that can be taken away from you by a bad business decision or relationship problem?

Sometimes, we have to lose everything, empty ourselves out before we can value the marvellous spiritual souls we really are underneath all the layers of camouflage. Emptying out the emotions, and even all desire, is a scary business. After I lost everything through a peculiar set of circumstances in 1995, I found myself sitting in an empty room, a symbol of my emotional emptiness. I was devoid of all identity, feelings and desires. It was certainly an odd experience.

This experience was very enlightening because we all put so much stock by our physical trappings and losing it all makes us realise what really matters. It changed me in a profound way that became clear only as time passed. I know now that I'm always okay no matter what my outside world displays. This offers the chance to operate from a position of great strength: once you've lost everything and survived, you can never be afraid of loss again.

Self-love means living without fear and replacing it with a deep-seated sense of peace. Like all love, it needs to be nurtured over time. We need to undo a lot of negativity every day from many sources around us that promote self-doubt and mistrust.

How men deal with emotions

There is a common myth that men are totally out of their depth with their feelings, especially the deeper ones. Myths are folklore and are often presented in the guise of truth, but just because a lot of people believe something does not make it true. I have seen just as many men as I have women in my counselling room who ache for real connection and long to open up with their feelings and needs. Women get to do this all the time with their women friends, family members and even their partners — if they're lucky — but who does a man go to? Also, women are trained to cope with their feelings and get on with their lives regardless. When a man encounters some really passionate feelings that he suddenly has to deal with, he usually hasn't had much practice so he either hides them — which he is certainly very good at out of necessity, or he falls apart.

Right now, many men are very angry because they feel they've lost their traditional roles, their importance and their women. When a man is angry, he usually deals with it in an overt and physical way, which only brings a negative reaction, and thus the whole cycle is perpetuated. Some of you are very confused and hurt. Unfortunately, coming out and plainly saying so is a no-no; therefore, you either disguise your pain under a cloak of anger or you withdraw altogether.

What I'm saying essentially is that you men lack training in how to feel and yet it is a most natural part of our human equipment. *Feeling* is perfectly easy; *expressing* emotion is an infinitely more intricate matter. Simply keep in mind what I have said throughout this chapter — *allowing* everything is the way to inner serenity and outward harmony. Celebrate everything that happens to you. If you lose ten dollars, say thank goodness it wasn't fifty; if you have to have a small operation on your foot, give thanks that it isn't more serious; if you have to work late, be grateful you have a job, and so on. Live your whole life in a spirit of thankfulness, even when someone hurts you or you're in a bad mood or you have a so-called problem to deal with. Gradually, your life will open up before your very eyes. (More on this subject in Chapter 11.)

A final word on emotions— never be ashamed of how you feel, express it as honestly as you can but try not to dump you feelings onto others, even the good ones, because your can only ever share joy, not force it on someone else.

It is through emotion that great works of art, children, music and many other joys of life are created but, as with so many other things discussed in this book, remember to be the boss. Runaway emotions can also be very destructive. There's no need for excess when your feelings are allowed to flow freely every day.

Positive self-talk

- I go within to look at my fears and overcome them.
- I stay in the moment and refuse to say 'what if' about the future.
- I reprogram myself on a positive basis.
- I learn to trust myself, and trust in others flows from this.
- I break the worry habit.
- I seek and own the true source of my anger and learn to release it in a constructive way.
- I respond to criticism as an adult, and then let it go.
- I love myself for what I am, not for what I have.
- I celebrate my life.

Chapter 5

RELATIONSHIPS

As childhood influences and relationships are covered elsewhere in the book, I'm going to concentrate in this chapter on discussing specific relationships and how to minimise stress within them.

I teach a university extension course called 'Relationships without stress', and on the first night, I always tease the group by telling them that I've brought them together on false pretences — there is no such thing as a relationship without stress! However, you can reduce the stress levels within a relationship in the same way as you deal with personal stress — by awareness, patience and balance.

Most of this chapter will be devoted to love relationships as they are the most challenging and difficult for most of us. Before I get into that vast arena, however, I will look briefly at family relationships and friendship.

FAMILY

The relationships you have with your family in adult life are largely a product of how you got along growing up. Throughout the book I refer to the effects on you of your childhood influences — the people who were in your world, the way your family related or didn't relate, the way you were spoken to, treated and touched, the things that you weren't given and so on. By the time you get into your late teens, your attitudes and beliefs are pretty well set until you actively choose to change or adapt them, and even then you can never change your basic nature which is a result of your genetic imprints combined with your early-life conditioning. There are literally layers and layers of beliefs at the subconscious level that you have to cut through if you are to reach your core self and make real connection. As we saw in Chapter 3, your core beliefs become the foundation of your life as an adult and you continually play out your behaviour patterns without even realising it. The first inkling usually comes when you are dissatisfied with one or more key aspects of your life and you decide to find out why you keep repeating the same mistakes and problems.

Once you start to examine your background and the things that happened to you when you were a child it may have an affect on your family relationships. I always like to warn clients that they may experience 'spontaneous recall' as a result of the counselling process. This is when thoughts, memories and feelings occur without warning and can bring tremendous surges of emotion as painful associations are triggered. It can in turn influence the way you feel about a parent who hurt you or a childhood incident you had long forgotten. Some adults remember in their later years horrific episodes of incest, verbal abuse and violence and when it is all brought out into the open, this brings a great deal of pain to the victim and the members of the family who were the perpetrators.

Many clients resist working on their past for fear of discovering something they can't deal with but I still maintain it is far better to remember and forgive than to just block out the memories altogether. There can be no healing in oblivion. Forgiveness must be specific and by choice.

It is perfectly natural for family relationships to alter in practical and emotional ways as children grow up, for instance when they are moving out, growing close, interacting less, starting their own families, or maybe moving to another town or state. The wise parent opens wide , the nest door and encourages their young to fly away; the more dependent, needy parent clings on and makes the whole inevitable process more painful for both parties. I talk about family relationships extensively in my earlier book, *Teenage stress*, and the key message was to love with open arms, to communicate openly and be supportive always. Those of you reading this who are parents, try to remember the things you hated being done to you and try not to repeat them. Unfortunately, so many family problems are perpetuated by generation after generation; in fact, it's often the things we hated most that we in turn do to our own children. Why? Because we want to heal. That's what all relationships are about — healing our pain. If we lived in an ideal world, we would all resolve our problems directly with the people involved but so often this is not possible and we end up working them out with other people who come into our lives. This will become clear when I talk about the laws of attraction in the next section.

Men are known to be poor at maintaining close family relationships. They tend to move out of home, get out into the world, meet their future partner and settle down or travel far and wide, dropping an occasional line to the folks at home. This will vary according to your individual natures and priorities but in general, I think it's fair to say that women stay closer to their families of origin after leaving home and even after starting their own families. Women are in fact often much closer to their mothers after becoming mothers themselves, whilst men separate the families they start from their families of origin. This can sometimes cause friction between their wives and their mothers where a natural rivalry often already exists. Men need to be aware of this and to try to take a more active role in keeping both sides happy. Their relationship to their wife is totally different from the one they have with their mother and obviously their new family must come first but there are simple and caring ways to be in the middle without being squeezed.

REDUCING STRESS IN RELATIONSHIPS

My general tips for reducing stress in relationships can be applied to all types of relationships — parents, siblings, grandparents, aunts and uncles, cousins, workmates, friends, in-laws, lovers, spouses. Here are the key tools required:

- effective communication
- assertiveness
- trust
- respect
- personal empowerment
- boundaries

Effective communication

As mentioned in Chapter 1, a key stress management tool is effective communication. How much more relevant is this when you're dealing with other people! Never assume that another person knows what you're thinking or feeling, and vice versa. So often in counselling I hear the statement, 'If my partner loved me, they'd know what I want.' Wrong! Point number one, you can never be sure that your perception of a situation is the same as another's, no matter how close you are, and point number two, it is not your partner's responsibility to guess what you want or what's troubling you. Be an adult and spit it out.

I have never counselled a couple who had good communication between them. If you can talk openly and honestly, without fear, there can never be an insurmountable problem between you. When I ask a couple if they talk together they usually protest that they most certainly do, but on closer examination it usually transpires that the conversation surrounds children, work, money and holidays, not feelings, hopes, dreams, and grievances. I recommend quality time every single day for couples whether they've been married a year or twenty and I don't accept the excuse of being too busy. Time must be set aside for free exchange, affection, silence, love-making, shared interests. Even if it's only half an hour, this ritual should become part of the daily schedule, a small oasis amidst the hustle and bustle of family life and busy routines.

Good communication and trust must work both ways. Some people are very good at dishing it out but are not so keen to be at the receiving end. I often find that one partner in a relationship is a better communicator than the other, or at least, keener and more willing. This has something to do with the polarities I mentioned in the previous chapter. We tend to pick people as lovers and friends who complement us, who appear to supply the missing halves of ourselves. If we could only realise that each one of us is a complete perfection just as we are, we would no longer have to go out in search of what we mistakenly think we need in another. When we accept all the parts of ourselves and learn to bring them out more and more, we will stop playing out polaric roles within our relationships, for example the husband who doesn't say a single word and the wife who never stops talking; one partner who makes all the decisions and 'wears the pants'; one who is a complete slob and the other compulsively tidy. Take turns at being everything and you won't have this problem. It happens because we are divided in ourselves and we're also a bit lazy about change, preferring to let our partners play out the opposite behaviour so we can criticise them for being too talkative or too untidy!

The very feature that attracted us most to our partners when we first met them is usually the thing that drives us crazy after a time together. It's as if we're saying, I loved and wanted those characteristics I saw in you when we first met but now that we're married or living together, I want you to start doing things my way. Let's face it — we all suspect deep down that our way is better! Try for acceptance. Talk over what's bugging you and ask for honesty in return. If you hear something you don't like, don't react negatively; promise to think about it and discuss it later.

Of all the complaints I get about men from their partners, poor communication is the biggest one — no contest. When I ask men why they don't want to talk over problems, they usually say they can't get a word in edgewise and their partner is making too much of the situation anyway. Surely there's a compromise here somewhere. Use some reverse psychology.

The more you resist something, the more attractive it becomes to the other person and the more persistently they'll pursue it. So try not to shut off or shut down. Always be open to listening and by offering solutions yourself you at least get to have some input. A little goes a long way. No-one likes to feel dismissed so try to resist telling your partner that her concerns are trivial and her opinions invalid; even if you believe they are, give them a hearing and offer constructive counter-arguments in a positive and loving way. This will enhance your relationship in ways that you won't believe.

Many a marriage has been destroyed by inept and indelicate management of problems. First, you have to be willing to communicate, then it is a matter of trial and error. Being able to ask instead of telling, learning how to apologise when it's fair to do so and being unafraid to speak your truth quietly — these skills are paramount. The ability to communicate effectively can arrest a problem before it gets out of hand. It lays down ground rules for relationship interaction, and is a key anger management tool.

Assertiveness

Another important skill is assertiveness. Most of us spend our early years being too passive, mainly because we seek approval. We think that if we come on too strong we will antagonise the people around us, even strangers. For males, maturity comes later — a guy of twenty-one is a much younger person than his female counterpart. By his late twenties, he is usually ready to take a more confident stance in the world and this is when he might notice the desire to keep everyone happy lessens. A pendulum never swings towards the middle. From being too passive, a man will become aggressive for a time, in line with his new-found self-image. He will start sending back meals that aren't right, speaking up if someone jumps him in a queue and generally standing up for his rights.

Assertiveness is the balanced position between the two extremes and it is a delicate and hard-won balance, probably the most difficult of all the life-skills because it's a bit like golf — you're only as good as your last game. Once again, the message is awareness — be aware of your own 'performance' regarding assertiveness, pat yourself on the back when you've done well and laugh it off when you don't succeed.

Here are the rules of assertiveness:

- Speak your truth quietly.
- Never stay to argue.
- Only say once what you wish to convey not twenty times.

You won't go from passive to assertive straightaway because newly-acquired skills feel very uncomfortable and when we are uncomfortable, stress levels are heightened. Once you have become accustomed to a new way of behaving, you no longer feel the need to prove it every minute. So when caught in an annoying or embarrassing situation, you can quietly speak up and change it, for example if you get a raw steak in a restaurant when you ordered well-done, you simply ask the waiter to return it to the kitchen. There's no need to shout or swear, which men do when they feel they need to prove a point or be noticed in some way. This is certainly not assertive behaviour, but instead, aggressive.

Why be assertive? Apart from keeping your stress levels and blood pressure low, it's a more effective tool for getting what you want. Have you noticed, people tend to listen more to a quietly-spoken person? In close personal relationships, I see that there's usually a shouter and one who is a 'passive-aggressive personality', in other words, quiet but angry and employing what I call the 'tyranny of silence', that is using silence as a weapon to hurt or manipulate. If both parties were to learn assertiveness skills, disputes could be settled with a lot less heartache and headache.

Assertiveness is a useful strategy for all types of relationships from home to workplace. In the previous chapter, I shared with you some conflict resolution skills that are handy for specific issues but assertiveness can be employed every day to resolve and prevent trouble.

TRUST

Reread the section on jealousy in Chapter 4 before you proceed here. Trust is like jealousy in that it comes from yourself, never the other person. Even if your partner appears to be provoking you to jealousy and to break trust, you always have the choice. You should trust someone because your instincts tell you you can and because you trust yourself. Never ask another if they can be trusted; if you have to do this and then watch and wait to see if you're right in your judgement, you may as well not bother at all.

As you read this, you might be thinking that you have trusted wholeheartedly in the past and been betrayed. Is that really true? Search your heart — is it not closer to the truth that you knew deep inside the person could not be trusted but you went against your own instincts anyway. Your intuition can never lead you astray but you have to practise listening to it. If you're in the habit of letting your intellect override your inner knowing, you will have to keep relearning the same lesson.

The converse is also true. You cannot ask another to trust you either; live in your own integrity and let them find out in their own time who you are. Many good and honest people are misjudged and mistrusted. That is the failure of the judge and not the judged. If you are doing what you believe to be right, fear the opinion of no-one. Only letting yourself down is a real sin.

Trust plays a pivotal part in close relationships and has to be total. It takes time to develop. Untrusting people have usually been let down in childhood or earlier relationships and thus fear opening themselves up to this risk again, but there is no risk when you follow your inner wisdom. Trusting blindly is just as unhealthy as not trusting at all, because if you're gullible and believe only the best in everyone you are indulging in wishful thinking. Of course there are people around who want to use you and will hurt you if you let them but it's your responsibility to avoid them, not theirs to be honest with you.

A client of mine married his wife after a matter of weeks, to find after a time that he was living with a stranger, a woman with character traits he could not accept, especially in regard to child-rearing. There is a natural passion period of about five to six months, during which time we can see no wrong with our partners. That is hardly the time to be making permanent commitments as thinking is clouded by lust and self-delusion. I could tell you many horror stories of such cases and perhaps you've experienced it yourself. If you have, you only have yourself to blame. Don't waste time and energy hating the other person — just acknowledge your mistake and vow to be more careful in the future. Without sincere trust, there can be no hope of a real marriage or relationship.

A knife-edge test of the kind of trust you need to sustain a long-term commitment is when an infidelity occurs. That will be covered in its own section in Chapter 8 but the point I want to make here is that even after a partner is unfaithful it's still up to your assessment of that person as to whether or not you can give her a second chance. If it was a genuine mistake, an aberration not to be repeated, then you were right about her in the first place but if you decide that your partner has changed and that she is no longer someone you can place your trust in, move on.

No-one can decide trust for you — it is one of the most misunderstood issues in relationships. It is closely aligned to honesty. A person honest in both word and deed is more likely to merit the trust of the people around him. Again I remind you we are mirrors. If we're not honest ourselves, we cannot hope to attract this quality into our lives. Heal yourself and all good things will come to you including trustworthy friends and lovers. If you feel that you're surrounded by dishonesty, look into your own background for the reason.

RESPECT

Respect is mostly to do with acceptance, that is to say, you respect the right of your partner, family member or friend to make choices of their own, be what they want to be, do things their own way, and so on. You do not have to agree with them; in fact, chances are high that you will not agree with your friends and lovers most of the time. I believe that some people are in our lives for joy and sharing and others are around to press our buttons and help us heal and learn lessons. The latter will generally be our more significant relationships, albeit the more painful ones.

Respect has to do with not judging or criticising. I think we have to be clear about this non-judgement. You are entitled to have opinions and preferences and you can even speak out about these but you do not have the right to pressure another or force them to accept your viewpoint. No-one can ever assess the rightness or wrongness of a situation for another no matter how close, because you are always going to see it from your perspective which is bound to be different.

If we could all accept without judgement, how much less complicated our relationships would be. This is particularly relevant to intimate relationships because it is in this arena that we feel most threatened by differences. Once again it is fear that spoils our joy. (We will speak extensively about sabotage in the next chapter.) Lack of trust, honesty and respect are three of the main ways in which we can sabotage our happiness. Most of us are scared that if we allow our partners total freedom, we will lose them, they'll fail us or something similar. Restricting someone or allowing them total freedom will not make a jot of difference to the way a person behaves. That person is either going to be faithful to you or not — you can't control everything.

Remember how we spoke of the need for control and how it comes from fear? You know the famous saying about loving something and setting it free — you can never own the thing you love, be it a person, thing or even a child or animal. With another adult you can only share, and with an animal or child it is only in your keeping for a time. It may be trite to say nothing is permanent but it isn't and by trying to hold on too tightly, you lose the very thing you seek to hold onto. Give everyone around you the respect you would wish for yourself and you can't go wrong.

PERSONAL EMPOWERMENT

Operating from a base of personal empowerment means being comfortable with yourself, clear on your own rights and living life assertively. In this position, you are much more likely to be happy, healthy and successful. Your relationships can be expected to work better as you're not working out your frustrations or expectations on another human being. Also, if you're empowered you're usually attracted to a like-minded person, so the incidence of co-dependence in the relationship is lessened.

Empowerment simply means acknowledging and honouring your own power — of mind, emotions and spirit. Once you do this, you will start to see it working in every area of your life every day. There's a lot more about this in Chapter 10 but it's worth mentioning it here in the context of relationships. Power struggles in relationships usually occur after the first flush of passion has died off and each party sees the imperfections of the other. There are distinct stages in a new relationship — romance, power struggle, crossroads, resolution, commitment. If we jump the gun and start committing ourselves at say stage two, we can easily make a mistake. I know this sounds unromantic but nothing is more unromantic than breaking up so keep to realism even through the 'violins and flowers' stage. When things start getting serious, the blinkers should be firmly removed.

In committed relationships, being clear on terms and conditions is essential to long-term happiness. Covering up your grievances only causes them to fester. That may sound too much like a business contract but after all that's what marriage basically is. Love should not be the only consideration either in choice of partner or whether you should get married or live together. It is only a beginning. There are lots of other factors that need to be taken into account. I'm a strong advocate of pre-marriage counselling because so many young couples get engaged without realising the full implications of the commitment they're making. After the wedding, even when the partners are fully prepared, comes all the hard work.

Marriage is the ultimate act of faith and is an ongoing experience that belongs to the two people involved. It must be a team effort and yet it's only as strong as its individual parts. Ideally, it is a union of two complete, happy, separate people who come together for sharing and enhancement of their life experience. You need all the advantages you can get to make it work and current world statistics tell us that we're failing to do so. (We'll look at marriage in detail in the next chapter.)

Holding your personal power, being aware of it and not abusing it, taking full responsibility for all your own needs, pains, desires, hang-ups, and so on will minimise the common faults in marital interaction that cause most break-ups.

BOUNDARIES

Establishing boundaries is one of the key skills for reducing stress in relationships and preventing marriage breakdown. There are three types of boundaries — sexual, emotional and physical. As the word implies, boundaries are barriers but, unlike walls, they are not defence mechanisms. They don't seek to keep the world out or prevent pain. They are healthy limits set by ourselves to make clear what we will and will not accept from the situations and people around us.

Sexual

A good example of an effective sexual boundary is not to have sex because you feel pressured to have it. This can so easily become a habit until you no longer even realise you're doing it. Sex should never be used as a power game or a way to pressure someone into what you need and want. No-one is alive for the sole benefit of another. Each party in any interaction must choose freely to participate for that relationship to be real. Women tend to complain more about this problem than men but, believe me, I have heard men say that they're tired of feeling that they must perform on request. Therefore, a healthy sexual boundary enables either party to say no without fear of rejection or creating dissent. Surely sex is an activity that engages the minds, hearts and bodies of two people and thus should be mutually pleasurable. If one partner has a much higher libido or interest in sex, compromises may be in order but these must still be mutually agreed to and freely given. (There are other factors involved in this issue which will be covered in Chapter 8.)

Emotional

Emotional boundaries involve not taking on board your partner's moods, not taking responsibility for another's insecurities and problems, dealing only with what is directly in your charge. That's not to say that you shouldn't care about others but caring is not care-taking. The latter suggests that you are trying to make it right for someone else and that can never work. Developing healthy boundaries will start to chip away at old feelings of obligations that belong to the past and other people. Do not give in to emotional blackmail and feelings of guilt that may come from parents or partners. With a mixture of self-esteem, assertiveness skills and healthy boundaries, you can deal with any unreasonable demands firmly but lovingly. It's like a ball-game — you need two to play. If you stop throwing the ball back, the game stops. So don't ask someone else to stop their behaviour — stop the game yourself by refusing to give in to pressure and insist on doing things only out of love, not duty.

Physical

This is the easiest boundary to understand and administer because it comes from the clear notion that only you are responsible for your own physical body and the space you occupy. That means you do not tell others what to do with their bodies or allow others to influence your choices. If you are in a physical situation you find uncomfortable you have to remove yourself, not ask someone to leave or change their behaviour. Every day of the week we find ourselves in situations we don't like, for example being crushed in a crowd, putting up with someone talking loudly in a movie or having our personal space invaded. I realise it was a lot more fun when we could attack and blame others for our discomfort but it's a lot more satisfying in the long-run to take personal responsibility.

If you're at a party or other function and you're not having a good time, do something about it or leave rather than complain that it's a rotten gathering or the other guests are at fault. You never have to stay in any place that doesn't please you — you always have choices. We always attract unpleasant situations when we are giving out negative energy so be aware of this.

Use boundaries in relationships of all kinds and you'll see how much smoother they are. Just keep your focus on yourself. You can never change another person — you can only change yourself. Whether at home, work, on the sporting field or at parties, there are always going to be situations and people that annoy you. If you let these irritants build up, imagine how much stress you'll accumulate over a period of weeks and months. Hold your own boundaries and learn the art of detachment. Most things are not worth worrying about. There's a very good saying that relates to this: 'Don't sweat the small stuff and it's all small stuff.'

Co-dependence

It seems appropriate now to move on to the very important subject of co-dependence. Healthy relationships operate on a system of co-creation — in other words, two people creating a relationship together that satisfies both and allows each autonomy, freedom and personal power. Co-dependence is the opposite. It is based on the assumption that there are two incomplete people who somehow need each other to become whole. It is an idea promoted by popular literature, music and folklore and is largely responsible for a lot of the unhappiness that exists in our society. People get married with this faulty concept and then they wonder why they become disillusioned. One partner is the 'propper' and the other the 'propped'. The relationship is based almost solely on need.

Sadly, most relationships are co-dependent and, amazingly, they're the ones that last! The cement that keeps people together in long-term relationships is usually mutual need. Previous generations accepted this as the norm but we have a lot more knowledge now and we want more from our relationships. Instead of staying and suffering, we break up. Have we gained or lost? I can't answer that for you personally but sociologically it has made a huge difference to modern life. I like to think we have more honesty in relationships on the whole.

Co-dependent relationships operate successfully until one partner changes. This may never happen but all too often it does and the other partner is left dazed and confused. Interestingly enough, it is usually the woman who decides she's had enough of a particular situation and goes out to do something about it. As long as both parties are playing out their designated roles, co-dependent relationships will continue. Remember polarities? All playing-out of polarities is co-dependent behaviour which simply means your needs match mine, so if I am compulsively tidy I will attract a slob I can nag at to shape up; if I'm a very quiet, shy person I will find a partner who is willing to talk for me; if I'm negative I can pair up with a positive person who gives me the opportunity to rubbish their optimism on a daily basis. If the other person didn't need the opposite effect, it wouldn't work — that is the key point. A good example is one involving an addict and his partner. Addicts don't like themselves very much and subconsciously seek abuse and punishment. If they knew this they wouldn't be in denial, which is a cornerstone of addictive behaviour. In order for an alcoholic or other addict to fulfil his co-dependence, he needs a partner who will supply the means by which he can feel like a terrible person. It's unlikely that this relationship would be sustained if the alcoholic were to stop drinking or the partner stop nagging and criticising.

This all sounds pretty grim but any problem in a relationship can be ironed out if both participants are willing to look at themselves and address the thorny issues. Addictive behaviour is escape, dropping out of life, and if it's continued for too long, even your most loved ones will not be able to follow.

Co-dependence is everywhere. I guarantee that every one of your relationships so far has been co-dependent. There are some tell-tale signs:

- working around others' moods
- feeling good only when the people around you are
- feeling responsible for others' happiness
- taking the blame for things that happen
- going along with what others want even when it doesn't suit you
- shouldering the burdens and responsibilities that belong to others
- feeling overloaded and playing the martyr
- laying guilt trips on others
- never being able to ask for help or admitting that you need anything
- caretaking others whether they need help or not
- preoccupation with others' needs and feelings
- disempowering others by taking away their choices and rights
- needing the good opinions of others in order to sustain self-esteem

These are just some of the key behaviours of co-dependence but in order to perform these roles, you need to find a willing counterpart who is also co-dependent. You cannot be co-dependent on your own. The word itself tells you this, *co* meaning together. A co-dependent relationship involves two people's needs that happen to dovetail and it operates on that basis. Getting out of co-dependence requires a lot of the skills already mentioned in the book so far — self-esteem, assertiveness, acceptance, personal empowerment. Working with these will increase self-love and a self-loving person does not need to lean on others for emotional sustenance or sense of identity. All good things that come from others are bonuses rather than necessities — love, companionship, affection, sharing, support, friendship. We never need to hunger for these things for they're always within us. We never need them from the outside. Imagine how liberating it is to live like that! If you choose to continue in co-dependent relations, you are in effect saying that you are incomplete without another person or group of people. It's your choice.

Once you become aware of how co-dependently you have related to others up to now you can consciously break out of your old patterns. It's very painful at times; along the way you have to let go of certain associations and discard people who refuse to function with you on a new level. Loved ones often associate lack of co-dependence with lack of caring because of their own personal history. But if you are sufficiently motivated you can do it, if you're willing to put in the work. This new way of living can apply to many areas of life. So many petty and joyless habits will disappear from your life because you'll no longer need them. You'll be able to praise yourself, honour your own feelings and fulfil your own needs. Look to others only for sharing.

All of the points I have raised in this chapter are applicable to a wide range of relationships, not only intimate ones. For example, there is plenty of mother–son co-dependence around. However, close alliances are the most challenging as well as being fertile ground for growth and learning. (These we will examine next in Chapters 6 and 7.)

Domestic violence can occur in any home in any relationship. Violence is a response to anger and frustration and can be just as addictive as anything else. I need not emphasise the need to seek professional help if you are either the victim or the perpetrator of violence in the home. It is not the solution to any problem or situation and in fact creates a whole new set of conflicts and difficulties. Don't wait till things get out of hand to admit the need for help. It is not at all humiliating to seek counselling or physical intervention but it is extremely demeaning to be chronically involved in domestic violence of whatever kind. Review the discussions of addiction, anger, respect and self-love.

There will be many factors of stress that I cannot cover in a book of this type which has to be general and broad in its scope. What I have tried to do, however, is to offer an overall strategy that you can apply to the various stresses that are pertinent to your life specifically, whether you are an incest victim, step-father, if you're dealing with learning difficulties, teenage children or your partner's PMT. As I have said throughout this book, the problem itself is only the manifestation of deeper issues so go no further than your own inner knowledge and use this book and others as a helpful guide for stress management and more positive living.

Positive self-talk

- I am open to listening.
- I apologise when I am in the wrong.
- I seek the balance between passivity and aggression.
- I look into myself before I blame others for a breach of trust or honesty.
- I allow others the right to their opinions and preferences.
- I acknowledge and honour my own power, and do not abuse it.
- I set reasonable boundaries, and respect those of others.

Chapter 6

BEING SINGLE

Love and marriage — do they really go together like a horse and carriage? Not these days, I'm afraid. Many couples are opting for a life together without a legal commitment, increasing numbers of men and women are choosing the single life, even long-term celibacy, and I notice a new phenomenon creeping in — couples openly declaring that they are not in love but want to share lives of companionship and friendship.

What is the message? The times they are a'changin'? We know that already. I think it's more like self-styling. As I stated in Chapter 1, the men of today do not necessarily want the same things as their fathers and grandfathers did, and that certainly includes relationships.

Before we look at marriage specifically in the next chapter, let's look at one of the common alternatives — being single.

THE SINGLE LIFE

Being single used to be seen as almost a curse, especially for women. It certainly was rarely a matter of choice and even in the 1990s there are single people who would much rather be in relationships but haven't met the right partner or can't make relationships last. However, there is a growing number of singles who are choosing to stay single as a way of life. Does this surprise you? I teach a university extension course for singles and over the past four years I have seen this trend grow. There are many misconceptions about singles, notably that they are undesirable, unattractive, desperate, lonely, weird, 'fussy' and perhaps gay. I have said already in the book that our society loves to label and we are suspicious of anyone we can't slap a ready label on. In our inadequate attempts to understand singles, we have come up with easy but inaccurate answers.

The singles who have attended my course are just as varied in age, appearance and personality as any other section of the community. Very few fit the stereotype. Many are bright and good-looking with great personalities. I ask them to examine society's expectations of singles and the standard labels and then discard them because we are all individuals before we're anything else. Having to deal with negative attitudes is one of the key disadvantages of being single. Other minuses include:

- difficulties of socialising
- not being invited to functions involving couples
- not having a special someone to share life with
- missing out on discount packages and bulk deals
- having to do everything on one income
- running a home solo

- threat of loneliness, feeling unloved
- lack of regular sex/intimacy

But there are just as many pluses:

- independence and autonomy
- more spontaneity/flexibility
- variety and scope of activities
- not having to consult another when making arrangements or plans
- more time for personal growth, hobbies and creative pursuits
- opportunity to focus more on career and professional development
- generally more choices and freedom

Being single is a viable life style and my strongest message to the group is to never wear the put-downs that marrieds might place on them, individually and collectively. There is no perfect way to be but you always have the choice of how you feel about it, for example if you feel less of a person because you are not in a relationship then that's your own low self-image. No-one else can ever really put you down if you have a strong sense of your own worth.

I always ask each class to raise their hands if they are committed to staying permanently single and out of a group of approximately twenty, only two or three hands will ever go up, which tells me that most people see the single state as temporary. That's fine as long as there is no desperation attached to waiting for their marital status to change. It's important to be happy in the moment whatever that moment might bring.

If you're single and don't want to be, keep putting forward that you want to meet someone and become part of a duo but enjoy the journey along the way. If you're miserable being single and you let everybody know it, you'll put people off. Be joyful in yourself and you'll attract all the love and companionship you want.

Being one half of a couple is no guarantee of happiness. All the good things about being married apply only if the relationship is happy. There is no lonelier place than a marital bed if you're not getting along. Marriage takes a lot more work than being single: you can please yourself most of the time when you live and operate alone. Yet most of us seek to join our lives with one other person, make a family and live together in a joint home. Both states can bring fulfilment if lived in a positive light.

You might be surprised to learn how many homes in Australia are single residences. There are lots of men and women living successful and happy lives by themselves. Here are some secrets for a happy single life:

- self-love and esteem
- looking after yourself sexually
- developing a social network
- taking risks and reaching out to others
- attending classes, courses, functions — keeping in touch
- seeing being single in a positive light
- joining clubs and groups to meet people, not just eligible members of the opposite sex
- refusing to accept labels or limitations
- enjoying being single even while continuing to look for a partner

We live in a couple-oriented society so, as a single, you will be part of a sub-culture but one that is growing and demanding respect as more and more people are insisting on making life choices based on suitability rather than tradition.

Contrary to popular belief, men do not as a rule enjoy being single. Putting aside gay men and perennial bachelors, males generally prefer to be with a partner. We can be cynical and suggest that the main appeal of marriage for a man is sex on tap and household chores done but, emotionally too, men like to be part of a family and often find marriage breakdown far more devastating than do women. Sure, a man is more welcome on the singles scene because statistically, the ratio of males to females in our society is far in men's favour. It's also easier for a man to socialise as a single: he can walk into a bar or club on his own and not be pointed out or stared at as a woman is. Also, society is much kinder in its assessment of male singles who are seen as elusive studs 'playing the field' whilst women are 'left on the shelf' and labelled 'spinsters' or 'desperates' if they've never married.

There seems to be some discrimination between singles who've never married and those who have been and are now 'between relationships'. If a man has not been married at least once in his life by the time he's forty, his sexual proclivity is viewed with some suspicion as people ask if there's something wrong with him. This happens too with men who have married more than once.

If you are out of a relationship and back on the single scene, especially if you're older, you will find that things have changed dramatically since you were last out there. Let's look at what you're up against now.

DATING

Not only have the rules changed, guys, the whole game is different, — I'm sure you've noticed! The biggest difference is in the attitude of women. Asking them out has never been easy for you; in fact, I've always thought that it's pretty unfair for the bloke to be the one who has to constantly lay it on the line and risk rejection. Nowadays you're just as likely to be asked out by a woman as the other way around. It may be a problem for your ego and take a bit of getting used to but why don't you just enjoy it? Who made these rules of courtship anyway, and where are they written in stone? I prefer to see men and women operating as equals and taking responsibility for their own social life, happiness and so on. If a woman wants to see a movie or eat out, why should she sit at home like a dummy, waiting for some guy she likes to phone and ask her? If I were a man, I'm damn sure I'd be flattered to be asked and grateful not to have to guess or not whether a woman is interested.

It's no longer assumed that a man has to pay for entertainments on a date, and bring flowers and chocolates. These are nice gestures but to me they've always smacked of a bribe. They certainly shouldn't be seen as obligatory. If a man wants to offer a small token as part of a night out, his date should just accept it graciously but by no means expect it or take it for granted. A good rule of thumb is, the one who asks should pay for dinner, movie or whatever but if it is a mutual decision to see a film together or attend a concert, they should 'go dutch'. If it becomes a regular thing, then the easiest solution is to take turns to pay.

Is chivalry dead and should it be? Do women want a man still to pull out chairs and open car doors? I believe the average woman still enjoys these gestures as long they are not done in a spirit of macho male–helpless female. A woman is perfectly capable of getting herself out of a car and seating herself but politeness knows no barrier of gender or age. I have often opened a door for a man struggling with parcels or picked up something he's dropped if he's overloaded. I see no conflict in this. I guess the message is to be sensitive to the woman you're dating.

Topics of conversation may vary from sport to personal issues but don't lay it on too thick on the first few dates. I've found from my experience of running groups over many years that men are often more bitter than women after a break-up so they tend to talk non-stop about the details of their marriage to anyone who will listen at social functions. The whole purpose of going out and meeting people is to move into the future, not relive the past, to share and exchange, not dump your troubles and hang-ups.

No matter what has changed, there is still the age-old question of sex: is it advisable on the first date, how to bring the subject up, who makes the first move and so on. My advice has always been the same — no sex on the first date unless sex was the only point of the date, in other words, there is no interest in pursuing a relationship on the part of either. (I will discuss one-night stands in Chapter 8. If however, it is a first date with the hope of a future, then sex too early kills it. Keep in mind the stages of a relationship mentioned in the last chapter. Jumping too soon into intimacy will only confuse the emotions as libido has a way of doing. You'll never know if the relationship is simply based on hormones because you didn't give it a chance to prove itself on other levels.

After a few dates, if you both feel that you want to go to bed with each other, either party can ask directly. If a partner is straightforward about sexual interest it eliminates a lot of game-playing and guessing. A woman is much more likely to respond favourably to an honest show of healthy lust than someone going all round the houses in pursuit of the same outcome. A man I was attracted to called in to my place and after a decent interval of conversation, said cheerily and without embarrassment, 'How about we go upstairs and get naked?' It was so disarmingly blunt that I had to say yes! I hasten to add for the sake of my reputation that he was someone I knew quite well, not a stranger. Nevertheless, the point remains.

It doesn't always have to be so outspoken, of course — it's better if sex happens naturally, as a consequence of good feelings between two people. But that might be asking too much after just a few dates. So go with your instincts and you can't go wrong. So often clients tell me they want to reach out, take a hand or offer a kiss but hold back out of fear, asking themselves is it too soon? What if she doesn't want it? What if I look a fool? And so on. There is no perfect way to gauge the signs — you sometimes have to let the moment lead you and take a chance.

These days, we have the added complication of serious health risks. There's a very 1990s joke doing the rounds about whether to introduce the subject of condoms before or after the cappuccino. My generation certainly didn't have to deal with such matters. Subjects like condoms and tampons were never brought up in polite company but now, we hear about them on television and the former are a very real fact of life on the dating scene. Even a person's sexual history is no longer private territory — we're supposed to ask each other about health risks and past lovers long before intimacy is even contemplated.

Yes, dating is a much more complex business than it has ever been in recent history. The very fact that there are so many more places to meet is in itself another complicating factor. Our parents and grandparents expected to marry the girl they dated, probably introduced by family or friends at a private home or church dance, certainly in the local town or village anyway. Compare that to the endless venues, methods and types of people involved in the dating process these days. The choice is limitless but it is no easier. It is one of the questions I am asked most by men in my work — how do I meet suitable women?

Surprisingly, younger men often find it more difficult to

put themselves out there as they lack the social skills and confidence necessary to meet and talk to women. Eventually, pubs and clubs lose their appeal and some men find it easier just to give up and stay lonely. Even clean-cut, nice looking chaps run the risk of being misunderstood in these places. They tell me they don't know how to behave — if they're cheeky and come on to women, they get knocked back or laughed at; if they're polite and keep their distance, they're treated like a brother or a 'mate'. Of course, it's the subconscious vibrations we give out that are responsible for a lot of these problems (more on these later in the chapter).

Pubs and clubs are not the best places to meet potential partners as they are designed for a good time and little else. Some guys use introduction agencies as a last resort, or advertise in the personals. These are okay as long as you choose reputable services and companies; shop around before you sign up and keep your expectations realistic.

In summary of this section on being single, the most important element is staying positive. If you allow yourself to become disillusioned and bitter, lonely and isolated, you will actually stem the tide of good fortune flowing your way. This will be made clearer in the next section about subconscious vibrations and how they dictate our life-course.

VIBRATIONS

We all talk about 'vibes' but what are they? They are waves of energy given off by our auras and they come directly from our subconscious self-images — in other words, what you see is not what you get. The outward personality that we present to the world is a mask, the 'persona' we have developed over the course of our lives. Much of what we really are and feel and want is hidden under many layers of self-protection and we convince ourselves that people are responding to the person we show forward. In fact, this is not the case at all. People respond to the vibrations we give out rather than the external behaviour we display. Here's an example.

You may take great pains to do your job well and please your boss but you never seem to get to first base. Others get promoted over you and your work is constantly criticised. You can't understand it. It could be that your invisible 'neon sign' is flashing: 'I'm not much chop. I'll let you use me as a whipping-horse.' That's the message your boss is reacting to and his treatment of you corresponds to his impression.

Here's a more personal example I hear from guys all the time. You're out at a party or pub — you're doing the right thing, buying drinks, being polite, listening intently, and at the end of the night, the woman you've been lavishing your attention on goes home with the cool guy at the bar who hasn't said a word or bought a drink all evening. Why? He has been putting out the right signals and you haven't. Probably his neon is: 'I'm sexy and I can give you what you want.' Your message could be: 'Don't worry about me. I'll buy you drinks all night and I don't want anything in return.' We give off signals about everything and they are directly linked to what we think of ourselves but not superficially, at a very deep level. Body language is simply non-verbal communication and it might surprise you to know that 85 per cent of all human communication is non-verbal. You can't govern body language. It expresses your hidden feelings, motives, beliefs, attitudes, values, and can be read by anyone who knows the codes. Through experts in the field, we have seen politicians for example revealing their real thoughts by their silent language and not what they think they're showing and saying.

Only subconscious changes will affect these vibrations so if you're not happy with the way you're being perceived, or the responses you're getting from others, resolve to make the necessary internal adjustments. It has to work from the inside out, not the other way round.

This is a very crucial area of relationships because it explains how we were attracted to our partners in the first place; therefore, by understanding it we can alleviate much of the relationship stress that causes conflict, quarrels and, eventually, breakdown of marriage. I want to now look at the laws of attraction and how they are linked to vibrations.

The laws of attraction

We think when we're attracted to someone that we like the look of their eyes, hair, features, or whatever, but in fact there is a subconscious pull that draws you to certain people for a variety of reasons. The two key reasons are:

- there's something you need to learn from this person, and
- she represents one of your parents

The parent this person represents is most likely your mother, not for gender reasons but because the mother–child relationship is the single most influential relationship any one of us will ever have in a lifetime. It colours every other relationship we subsequently have. Whichever parent you have unresolved issues with is the one you will (subconsciously) seek in a partner. You will not be aware of this and you may be in denial over what it is you need to resolve in the first place. That's why so many of us end up with the wrong people. We choose blind, coming from past unhealthy impulses instead of self-love and clarity. Again, I run the risk of sounding unromantic but personally, I prefer to make informed choices rather than rush in without thought and 'repent at leisure'.

To understand this section fully, you might want to reread the section on core beliefs in Chapter 3 as they are directly related. As I explained then, we hold core beliefs about everything. For now, the relevant ones are those about love, marriage and home. What you saw when you were growing up forms these beliefs and you act them out unconsciously until you bring them up to the surface. Let's take some specific examples. Whatever you understand love to be, unreliable, lovely, risky, guaranteed to hurt, a trap, designed to take away your freedom — the options are endless — you will go out into the world expecting exactly this. So, if you think love is a trap, for instance, you will probably be 'commitment-phobic', which means that you will avoid being tied down in any way. This can be achieved in a number of ways. You can simply stick to superficial encounters, you can break up as soon as you start getting too close to someone or you can stay away from love altogether. You won't know why you make these choices; you'll just go on acting them out. A person who responds to love in this way is also known as an 'avoidance addict', which describes a desire to run away from deep commitment and feelings of real intimacy. 'Love addicts' on the other hand are hooked on the idea of love and hold a fantasy picture of what it means. They usually go from lover to lover seeking the realisation of this fantasy which of course can never become reality. As with other forms of addiction, these two involve handing over one's power and the search for fulfilment through an outside source. They can bring nothing but frustration and pain.

Love addicts usually come from emotionally deprived backgrounds and avoidance addicts typically have experienced the opposite — they felt emotionally suffocated as children so panic at the thought of being loved as adults. 'Cut and run' is the usual response.

Relationship patterns

I can offer only a few examples of relationship patterns in the scope of this book but if you relate to any of them, you'll know what I mean and hopefully will recognise your specific pattern. To me, this is the most crucial piece of information you need in your relationship equipment kit. It's the first exercise I give my students in any relationship course I teach. Until you know your pattern, you cannot make any changes or improvements to the way you relate.

So how does this pattern affect you when you meet someone? Well, the first rule is: the woman you're instantly attracted to is the one you should run a mile from! She's the one who's most likely to hurt you if you go further than a date or two. It might sound boring but the recipe for a long and successful relationship is to start with friendship, have a long courtship, keep those hormones in check for a few months and build a foundation for love to grow. However, seeing that most of you will not heed my advice on this, I had better tell you what to expect if you follow the instant attraction. There are basically two types of vibrations that come into play when you meet someone. Remember I talked about the intuitive reactions you sometimes feel to people when you sense an immediate like or dislike for no apparent reason. Well, the principle is the same whether it is a positive or negative response — something about that person is pressing your buttons. As a man, you might be far more aware of a woman's body or smile or the size of her breasts but the 'pull' you feel is subconscious and linked to your past history and your patterns.

If the vibration is a 'matching' one, you are being drawn to a woman who has a belief system that matches yours. Here's how it works. Think back to the example I gave of believing that love traps you. If this is your core belief about love a woman with a matching vibration will be offering love that traps you. Get it? She's offering to fulfil your expectation of what love is. Of course all of this is unconscious and unspoken. You may not realise for years that you have fallen into exactly the relationship you most feared. If the woman is overtly clingy and demanding you would run a mile, but people don't usually show their true colours in the first few encounters; hence the need for time and caution. If you saw your mother 'trapped' at the kitchen sink, giving up her dreams or being treated as a second class citizen, you're quite likely to turn around and behave the same way towards your wife; if you saw your father hen-pecked, nagged and unhappy, you may well end up being the same kind of husband.

You're probably asking yourself why anyone would wish to repeat the unhappiness they saw in their parents' marriage — because it's what you know; it's your core belief. The clearest examples of this occur in extreme cases of abuse. Why do women who had violent fathers marry wife-beaters? Why do women marry womanisers if they had fathers who were chronically unfaithful to their mothers? Why do guys with dominating mothers marry bossy women? There is no mystery; in fact, if you look at it, it makes perfect logic. You are responding to a matching vibration when you 'fall in love' with these particular people. You can't help it, you say? Oh, yes, you can. You just have to choose with your instinct and your conscious mind and not your libido and your subconscious mind.

With an 'opposing' vibration, you are attracted to a person who breaks your pattern, who is going to offer you the opposite to what you expect. Unfortunately, as I explained in the section on co-dependence, the noncodependent relationships are the ones least likely to last. Again, it's easy to understand why. Someone who breaks your pattern makes you feel very uncomfortable. It's like wearing shoes that don't fit. Eventually, being so happy starts to terrify you! It makes you feel too vulnerable; it's too risky; it doesn't feel emotionally safe.

When we can't find a logical reason for our feelings, we make one up! It's called rationalisation and seeks to give reason to our irrational choices and behaviours. So if you're in a relationship with a woman who's offering freedom with mutual respect and sharing (to use the same example) and you expect love to trap you, you will break it off even though you may be very happy; in fact, because you are. How sad do you think it makes me to have to stand in front of a class or write in a book like this that we human beings are so lousy at being happy? In a co-dependent, unhappy alliance, you will feel more at home and stay on even if it hurts; when a woman offers a break away from the pain of the past, you run scared. If you're thinking as you read this that you haven't been guilty of this behaviour, that you had good reasons for breaking off with various women, think again. The psyche is very adept at fooling itself and convincing itself of what it needs in order for you to sleep at night. It's much easier to believe that you broke off because you didn't like a certain habit or physical feature of a woman, or a member of her family, or some other trivial thing, than to deal with the deeper reason. What I'm saying is that until you go within, identify your pattern and seek to break it, you're doomed to keep repeating the same mistake; worst of all, you won't know why.

A young client of mine consulted about this exact problem. He was only twenty-four but he could see that he had a definite pattern of behaviour in his relationships. He could date a woman for only about four to five months and then he would feel an irresistible urge to break it off for some minor reason or other. Naturally, he was worried that he would never be able to have a lasting relationship unless he could work out why he was doing this continuously. It transpired that when he was fourteen, he was madly in love with a girl at school. They went out together for about four months, and he was very happy but suddenly, without warning, she broke it off. He was devastated, absolutely heartbroken. Somewhere deep inside him, he probably vowed never to feel that way again so his subconscious mind took over every time he got to like a girl and when it got to the four to five crucial month period, he jumped in first and broke up. This kept him safe from ever having a woman leave him again.

Doesn't it make perfect sense? The only problem is the pattern becomes entrenched and you're a slave to it without even knowing why. Knowledge is power, they say, and certainly in a case such as this one, once the client understands what he's doing it's as if a light bulb goes off and the pattern is broken. My job resembles that of a detective — I have to ferret out the clues and let them lead me to the answers which hopefully bring healing and change.

Falling in love is heady stuff and none of us would want to give up those first magical feelings that transport us into a world that is brighter and happier than our usual existence. All I ask is that you do not forget that love has little to do with these early chemical reactions and hormonal stirrings. Love is something else altogether and if you kid yourself at the beginning, you will be settling for a facsimile instead of waiting for the real thing. Real love requires much more effort, commitment and personal courage but there is still nothing in this world as wonderful as feeling totally connected to another human being emotionally, spiritually and sexually. Perhaps some of you have never allowed yourself this joy either because of fear or cynicism or because you are blocked by old patterns. Well, now you are being offered the tools to do something about it.

What you give out in your vibrations return to you in the form of reflections. This is where I suggest you begin. Look around you and see what your life is reflecting. See Chapter 10 for details. In terms of relationships, reread Chapter 2 about identity and the responses you get from others. Listen to the complaints and criticisms of those you're closely involved with for they have a lot to teach you. Put aside arrogance as that is a limitation. If five people tell you you have a particular character flaw, it's unlikely that they're all wrong so look at it and try to come up with a strategy to improve that part of yourself.

The key is to be unafraid of your 'shadow' self, the dark side of your personality. We all have one and it's healthy as long as we incorporate it into our whole selves and not reject it or hide from it.

Positive self-talk

- I acknowledge that the way I feel about being single is my own choice.
- I refuse to accept that there are insuperable limitations to being single.
- I review my belief systems because they determine the non-verbal messages I give out.

Chapter 7

MARRIAGE

Having looked at what it means to be single, the particular pecularities of dating in the 1990s and what makes us choose certain people, let's turn now to relating to each other, the key stress traps and why some marriages work and others don't. Remember that a lot of general skills offered for relationships are applicable to marriage as well and I use the term 'marriage' to include any long-term committed relationship. As already stated, there are so many variations these days but each is valid as long as it suits the particular couple involved.

COMMON PROBLEMS AND STRESS TRAPS

In most close relationships such as marriage you are likely to find problems that will contribute to stress. Following are some typical areas of difficulty:

- projection
- poor boundaries
- boredom and staleness
- individual psychological problems
- emotional immaturity
- stress/tension
- sex
- cultural, religious and political differences
- poor health
- poor life style habits
- alcohol and other addictions
- family and friends
- guilt and retribution
- infidelity
- communication difficulties
- children and parenting
- money

Projection

We all enter new relationships with excess baggage from the past, be it childhood experiences or previous love affairs. It's terribly important to resolve and release these old hang-ups before we enter into a fresh commitment; otherwise we just repeat the same behaviours. While few of us ever become so enlightened that we stop acting out hang-ups and carrying personal hurt it is essential that we do not 'project' where in we not only dump onto our partners our own problems, insecurities and beliefs but we attribute them to the other person. It's more than laying blame; we usually believe the other person is guilty and behave accordingly. For instance, if you were beaten as a child you accept this as normal — unless you have backlashed and gone the opposite way. For the purpose of this illustration, let's say you tend to act out your frustrations with your fists and your temper because that's what you saw your father doing. If you follow your pattern all the way, you will marry a woman who will allow you to hit her but in order for you to do so you have to believe that your behaviour is justified. You'll maybe project onto her characteristics of your mother that drove your father crazy or you'll watch for some trait you disliked in a previous lover and imagine you see it in your wife. This is just the most obvious type of projection. Some forms are far more subtle and sinister and therefore much more difficult to detect.

Projection is one of the most destructive behaviours in marriage and one to really watch for. Every one of us is guilty of it to a greater or lesser extent and the only cure is being prepared to deal with one's own issues without seeking a scapegoat. Blaming another just clouds the whole situation and lets us off the hook of personal responsibility.

Poor boundaries

We have already looked at boundaries and I've explained the importance of these in maintaining good personal relations as well as remaining at peace with yourself.

Boredom and staleness

This kills off more marriages than you might realise. People are often too lazy to look at ways in which a relationship might be freshened up and kept exciting. It's easier just to look elsewhere for another partner or an illicit love affair. Boredom can find its way into the bedroom very easily once it has set in elsewhere. If you're bored with each other out of bed, it's quite likely you'll start losing interest in sex as well. Sex in marriage is different from sex elsewhere as I'll be examining in Chapter 8 – it can get stale because of its availability but also because other stresses interfere in the marriage.

To prevent a relationship getting dull set aside quality time every day that is for each other alone. When there are children this can be difficult, but it can be done. I have heard of some very creative measures being adopted by couples who are juggling careers, parenting, everyday routines, personal interests and so on. If you really want to keep your marriage alive, don't let the romance die, guys. I'm not suggesting you have to wine and dine your wife and spend heaps of money doing it. It's more a case of attitude and little thoughtful gestures such as occasional flowers or a small gift, but far more importantly, really listening to what she has to say. Women often complain they don't get enough of this. Be affectionate, not just sexy! Do little things to please her and make her feel special. A woman wants to know she's still desirable to her husband, not just by a regular grope in bed but in a meaningful way: be interested in her problems and plans; do things together; be thoughtful in little ways.

Communication is a key tool here: if you're communicating poorly, or not at all, it's hard to turn on at bedtime. There's another well-known myth that men are always ready to have sex, no matter what else is going on in their relationship. You'll see in the next chapter that I don't believe this. Male sexuality is different certainly and operates differently but men are just as sensitive to hurt feelings, moods and other factors that affect sexual interaction.

Sex is certainly one way to keep marriage exciting but equally important is honest communication, romance and quality time. With all these components present, you'll stand a good chance of keeping your relationship vibrant and constantly evolving.

Individual problems and emotional immaturity

We have already discussed how each partner's background and personal psychology play a part in the way two people interact in a relationship. That's why, before entering a serious commitment, it's so important to deal with your own issues, whether they be unresolved childhood pain or leftover problems from previous love affairs.

We also saw how often we project our beliefs and hang-ups onto partners instead of having the courage to look honestly at our own behaviour. Much of the stress in relationships comes directly from an individual behavioural problem, be it addiction, anger, poor boundaries or a communication difficulty. When couples consult me, I have to first ascertain whether the problems they report are actually of a marital nature. Very often, I have to suggest that one or other of the partners needs individual therapy before we can address the difficulties within the marriage. It's relatively easy to tell whether this is so after a few years' experience as a counsellor. It's not a matter of apportioning blame, but if a wife or husband is dealing with a personal problem it has to impinge on the relationship. Conversely, we sometimes blame outside influences such as in-laws, job stresses or financial worries for relationship clashes when the problem is in the relationship itself. As an impartial observer, I can make practical suggestions for change, but only if the person involved is prepared to do the work without denial or defensiveness.

Men sometimes feel discriminated against in counselling situations, feeling that therapists automatically take the female's side. I think on the whole men don't like seeing counsellors, again for reasons of social conditioning connected with sorting things out for themselves. Yet, as I say in my introduction, men are far more committed to the process once they make up their minds to go through it. I guess it all comes back to how much you really value the relationship. No-one likes being told they have problems to work out but if you can get past fear and ego and pride and look at how much you have to gain, you can be liberated once and for all from the demons of your past.

Stress/tension

As this whole book is about stress, I will simply emphasise again that stress can cause emotional distress which adds to relationship problems and, in turn, relationship problems cause stress. Therefore the simple answer is to live within comfortable stress levels and to distinguish between your own personal stresses and the stress of the relationship.

Some relationships are more volatile than others, more passionate, more argumentative and challenging. This is often the case when feelings run very strong, so it's up to the two people involved to find constructive ways to minimise the tension and conflict. Much of relating to each other is about compromising and give-and-take anyway. You can't deal with your partner's stress levels but you can ensure that yours are healthy so that you don't add extra pressure to the relationship.

The same rules that apply to managing personal stress can be applied to relationships — balance, a sense of humour, self-love, respect for yourself and the other, releasing tension in positive ways, keeping yourself fit, good communication. This whole chapter and the previous one describe relationship stress, how to prevent it as much as possible and how to alleviate it once it becomes evident. These chapters and the very first chapter of the book offer a blueprint for you to make your own life less stressful and operate less stressfully within all your relationships.

Sex

All of the next chapter is devoted to this subject but I'd like to cover the subject of marital sex here. As I implied earlier, sex in marriage is different. I wrote an article a few years ago called, 'Sex and marriage — do they always go together?' You might think that's an odd question but in fact there are a lot more celibate marriages around than you might imagine — couples who choose to stay together but have drifted away from any intimacy with each other. There are couples who take extra-marital partners regularly but still stay married, and couples who have an actual arrangement to live without sex in their marriage.

There are a variety of reasons for these arrangements and I say good luck to them if they are happy. It's the couples who are bitterly unhappy in the bedroom and who want to change but don't know how that concern me.

Why is sex in marriage different to casual or single sex? By its very definition, it's less sexy. Maybe not at first but after one or two years even the most loving couple can feel jaded. Sex that's always easily on tap becomes routine if you're keeping to much the same format, positions, time and place. It's difficult to ravish each other in the middle of the lounge-room when you have a toddler running around, and at the end of a long day you don't have the energy or the inclination for bedroom gymnastics. So often it's a quickie and off to sleep.

Married couples also take to bed with them not only their bodies and their libidos but all the issues and stresses of the day. Could you imagine being out on a casual date and in the middle of a passionate kiss, being asked, 'Did you remember to hang the hand-washing out?'! Yet couples who live together have a lot of these realities to contend with — financial problems, work worries, kids, plans, decisions, chores — not very sexy is it? Fatigue is another turn-off. By eleven o'clock at night you've usually had enough of all the demands of the day. Men complain that they don't always feel like 'performing' when they've been out selling or working at a desk or plying a trade all day; women tell me that sex often feels like the last chore of the day if it's expected every night.

Sex is one of those things in life that are very natural and simple till they go wrong. Then the stress of maintaining the pretence or taking a stand and fighting about it becomes intolerable. A lot of the general information in Chapter 7 will help in this area, but remember to make allowances for the fact that if you're married you can't expect sex to be mind-blowing every night. You need to respect your partner's feelings and never apply pressure for sex. Finally try to find a variety of ways to be intimate so that sexual intercourse is not the be-all-and-end-all.

The best time to have sex is when you're both feeling good, preferably after a romantic, relaxing evening out together. Even if you can't go out because of money or kids, set up a special evening at home with a beautiful table, wine, flowers and music, and make love as a natural flow-on from the loving mood you have created. Take a bath together, massage each other, make love in the shower. Variety and fun are the catchwords. Anything that becomes routine and expected loses its lustre.

Guys, be affectionate, not as a prelude to sex but just for the touch and the intimacy. Women love to be stroked and caressed in non-sexual ways and if they feel that every time their husbands hug them it's going to mean a visit to the bedroom, eventually they rebuff the advances and the rot starts setting in. The little things add up so try to become more aware. You men tend to like things simple — it's not that you mean to be insensitive. Remember that women are a lot more complex and somewhat less obvious so you need to watch for subtle signs that things aren't right or that your partner wants more tenderness. If communication in general is difficult, it's a hundred times more so in bed. Many men and women find it hard to express their desires and say straight out what they want or would like. It takes time and trust which is what marriage is all about. What marriage loses in spontaneity and excitement, it gains in intimacy and depth of feeling. I think marital sex is the most exciting sex of all because of its emotional component and the opportunity it offers for experimentation.

If you're finding your sex life stressful, try to be clear in your mind where the stress is coming from — has it got to do with your attitude to it or the amount of sex you're having, or are you with an incompatible partner? Once you have this information, you can do something about it. Take responsibility for the way you feel about sex and remember that, as with everything else in your life, your sexual preferences and values didn't develop in isolation. They are the result of your upbringing and the core beliefs you formed in childhood. If you heard your father speaking in derogatory terms about women, that will most probably be your view as an adult. Our parents are our gods until we grow up and realise that they too have feet of clay, but by then our beliefs and behaviours are firmly entrenched.

Don't waste energy blaming your partner when things aren't right in the bedroom. If the cause is clearly coming from an outside source, such as an overloaded schedule or a family problem or financial shortage, then try to eliminate its influence on your sex life. If, however, it is more deeply rooted, as many of our sexual hang-ups are, get professional help: it won't go away by itself. If it's your partner's issue, unfortunately, you can only be patient and recommend that she seek help. Most importantly, never criticise or apply pressure because those are the biggest turn-offs of all. Fighting about sex or demanding improvement will simply cause the stress levels betwen you to accelerate and the problem to spiral until it is bigger than both of you. As with all stress management, prevention is always preferable.

Cultural, religious and political differences

I've combined these issues as the principle behind each is much the same. If we take first cultural differences, there is a law in psychology called the law of propinquity. It governs the need in each of us to be drawn to those of similar kind and within geographical reach. A very clear example of this occurs when a marriage partner is unfaithful and so often it's with a neighbour, close friend of the family or even an in-law.

In counselling, I am asked why, why, why and I am told that it adds so much to the pain when infidelity happens with a person known to the spouse. Of course it does but it's caused by the law of propinquity. Unless a man is a chronic womaniser or a woman is a raving nymphomaniac, the average person does not go out to look for extra-marital sex. If it happens it's usually because it's right under their nose, with someone already around, perhaps an attraction that's always been present but dormant.

This same rule applies to all romantic attraction. We tend to go to the same places, mix in similar social groups and date people from familiar cultural and racial backgrounds. Even within the multiculturalism of Australia, inter-racial marriages are still in the minority. I don't believe that we should ever let differences get in the way of real love but realistically marriages between people of different nationalities, religions, countries and language do pose extra challenges. They require more tolerance and patience. Sometimes it's not the two partners themselves but their families, who disapprove of their children's choices. I know of a case where a Malaysian woman was unable to introduce her boyfriend to her family because he was too white! Bigotry works both ways and is found in many forms.

Cultural differences can certainly add a good deal of stress to a relationship but not if you apply the same general rules of respect, communication and trust. Acceptance of difference is a key factor of a healthy marriage.

Religion just by itself is a highly volatile subject and whilst you might be able to avoid it at dinner parties, it's impossible to ignore your partner's beliefs if they are very strong and affect the everyday reality of your marriage. It's one thing to go to separate churches on a Sunday but what if your wife is Jewish and wants to have a Sabbath ceremony in your house every Saturday? What if she belongs to one of the apostolic churches and has to attend services twice on a Sunday and on several week nights? What if you can't agree on the religion your children will grow up in? These are just some obvious dilemmas. Either one of you converts to the other's faith or you have to agree to not interfere at all with each other's religious practices and beliefs. Otherwise, it's a recipe for disaster.

Political differences often involve deeply held ideological differences such as those based on equal rights in marriage, gender roles, even having children. These can be sensitive issues that reflect values brought from family backgrounds or different education. It is important to understand and respect the other's point of view to avoid stress.

Poor health.

Please see Chapter 9.

Poor life style habits

Refer to Chapter 1.

Alcohol and other addictions

Alcohol is one of the single most destructive factors in long-term relationships. (See the section on co-dependence in Chapter 5.) If you have an addiction and you are married, or your spouse is an addict, your marriage will either have to be co-dependent or you will both have to be extra, extra committed to making it work. Once you understand the true nature of addiction (see Chapter 8), you will know that it usually stems from an underlying cause and has little to do with the people around you. Unfortunately, it's those closest to you, the ones you love, that are the most affected.

Alcohol is one of the more obvious addictions and very negative in its manifestation as it often changes the personality of the drinker, bringing on violence, aggression, sentimentality, loudness and argumentativeness not usually seen in the person. However, there are many other, more subtle forms of addiction that cause as much harm in relationships. You can be addicted to almost anything from a chemical to a food to a way of behaving, and you are the only one who can choose to break the power this has over you.

Keep in mind that your partner and the rest of the family are also in the grip of your addiction. There's no way to keep them totally apart. Even secret addictions like gambling negatively impinge on those around you, and when eventually all comes to light you'll find you've lost the trust of those you love. Very often families break up over alcohol and other forms of addiction. If they don't there is a lot of pain and unhappiness for all concerned. I don't mean to paint a gloomy picture but it's my responsibility to be accurate and realistic. Addictive behaviour goes hand in hand with denial and avoidance so you need to get past these first if you are to break your patterns.

If your partner is the addict, again I can only say give your love and support but do not feed the addiction in any way. Refuse to participate in any power games or accept any responsibility for the addictive behaviour. You may think you're helping but propping an addict up is an unloving act. While it might give you a more peaceful life it will keep the relationship in denial.

Family and friends

When you marry someone you take on their family and friends and vice-versa. There is no rule that says you have to love or like them but, unfortunately, if you want an equitable and harmonious relationship you have to accept them. Here are some of the common stresses associated with this area:

- in-laws who don't like the family member's choice
- interfering parents, particularly mothers
- disagreements about how much time should be spent with friends/mates
- family/friends being around or calling in too much
- different family styles
- ex-partners being around

Assertiveness skills are paramount here. Refuse to allow your parents, family and friends to influence your choice of partner, to criticise the person or interfere with your relationship. Firmly make it clear that you like your girlfriend and that's what counts. Always put your partner first without actually taking sides if there is a dispute. Absolutely refuse to allow your family to be rude to your partner but don't let rifts develop that might lead to separations or people not speaking to each other. Give respect to all parties, and demand it in return,

Set ground rules with your partner about time spent with friends, whether it be your drinking buddies or her girlfriends. I am one hundred per cent in favour of separate friends and interests. These help to keep the marriage alive and interesting. One or two days or evenings apart won't do any harm at all, probably the opposite. If you love sport and she loves the opera, why should you each have to endure the other's interest? Isn't it better to go with a companion who also enjoys that activity? If one of your wife's girlfriends calls in, let the two of them talk together privately. I can never understand couples who have to be tied at the hip all day. This is all right in the first year or so of marriage and certainly during the courting stage but once you're married and established, trust and space become more valuable commodities. After you've been apart for a while, you'll appreciate each other that much more. Obviously, if one or both of you have friends that abuse their visiting privileges by calling in too often or at inappropriate times, the one whose friend it is must point out that this is not going down very well and ask for an adjustment.

Differing family styles can cause stress through misunderstandings and hurt feelings if there is poor communication. For instance, some cultures are naturally more stoic and reserved, such as Germans and Scandinavians. They are not always very accessible on meeting and can even appear unfriendly. If you happen to be dating a woman from one of these countries, and are introduced to her family, you might think they don't like you because of their manner. If this is explained to you there's no problem as you can take your time and get to know each other. The opposite case applies with Latins such as Italians or Portuguese who are much more exuberant and demonstrative and may overwhelm someone unused to this style of interaction. Many other factors come into play such as noisy interplay at family gatherings, the level of disclosure that people feel comfortable with, the sharing of stories that may bore an outsider, and so on.

The same applies to demonstrating affection. If you've come from a family that does not openly show affection, you might not appreciate being hugged and grabbed at the first visit by an aunt or cousin of your partner's.

It's just a matter of communication and yes, acceptance that we're all different and there's no right or wrong way to interact. Just be patient if something happens that you don't like. Either they'll get the hint or you'll get used to it! In extreme cases, you might have to speak up but it's usually the small things that drive us mad at first.

Guilt and retribution

When we've been hurt, it's very natural to want to punish the offending party and there are many ways to do it. You can employ what I call the 'tyranny of silence', that is using silence as a weapon to hurt back or 'not speaking' for protracted periods of time, creating tension and making your displeasure clear. There are more obvious methods such as arguing, shouting, hitting, threatening, accusing, blaming and bullying; more insidious tools to use are emotional blackmail, power games, psychological warfare, manipulation, and projection.

None of these is a healthy choice. We spoke about guilt in Chapter 4 and saw that it is often irrational and based on low self-image. Just as it can eat into your self-esteem and damage your confidence, so it can corrode the fabric of a relationship. It is the basis of a lot of co-dependence because if I can make you feel guilty I can get you to do things that I need and want from you. This sort of manipulative behaviour only works with the unaware and, again, it is commonly a weapon used by addicts to take the heat off themselves. Don't participate in guilt games. Accept only what is your responsibility in the relationship and place the rest of it squarely where it belongs — with the other person.

If you are the one who likes to lay guilt, look into yourself for the real motive. What are you trying to cover up? We all tend to blame others for our failures and unhappiness. It's something we seem to learn in the schoolyard and it's all tied in with the fear of being in the wrong ourselves, covering up our misdemeanours, not getting found out. That's okay for the child but the adult faces responsibility and accepts the consequences of his or her actions and choices.

If you can do that, and insist that those around you do the same, you can't go wrong.

Infidelity

We'd all agree that this is a 'biggie'. Whether you've done it or been at the wrong end of it it's an extremely painful experience, and nine times out of ten leads to relationship break-up. Statistically, men are more often the adulterers but women are certainly capable of being unfaithful. Could I say at the outset that it is not the worst marital crime and should not automatically lead to separation and divorce. While millions of women would disagree with me I consider betrayal of other kinds to be just as damaging as sexual infidelity. Of course you are breaking your marriage vows and risking the trust of your partner but what counts most is your motive. Have you ever done this before? Did you set out deliberately to be unfaithful? Was it an aberration or something you're likely to repeat?

The worst aspect of infidelity is the deceit involved. There are many debates about whether it's better to tell your partner if you've had a one-night stand or have fallen for another woman. Whilst I don't accept the excuse of 'I didn't know what I was doing', if it was genuinely a one-off event that happened in a moment of weakness it's probably better to say nothing and learn from the experience. If, however, it looks likely to continue beyond a quick roll around in the sheets, then I think trying to have your cake and eat it too is pretty reprehensible. I can't decide your moral code for you but if you are serious about preserving your marriage, honesty is the best policy.

In a perfect world, we would all be up-front about everything, would never be afraid to come clean and would forgive each other totally. Unfortunately we don't live in a fairy tale and feelings do get hurt and marriages are wrecked by infidelity and dishonesty. All you can do is take your chances, own up and hope that your relationshp is strong enough to come back from such a difficult test.

I have seen relationships made stronger and better from such a testing struggle but there has to be a great deal of love and forgiveness present for it to work. Also, it's no good the 'wronged partner' saying all is forgiven if it's going to be brought up at every opportunity in the future. The American psychologist, Irene Kassorla, says we all have an 'anger shelf' where we store the grievances from past quarrels and our partners' misdemeanours. When we're angry, we bring everything down from this shelf and throw it up. How chillingly true and how very unhelpful.

If you have been the victim of infidelity, decide if whether or not you can really forgive with a pure and whole heart. Forgiving may not mean forgetting but if you remember too much it will interfere with the relationship to a point where all trust is corroded and the offending party can't put a foot right. Guilt is an unsavoury bed companion.

As hurtful as it would be to think of someone else making love to your partner, I would be much more interested in knowing why it happened. Was there a failure in the marriage itself? Did the person who strayed feel neglected or unloved? Was communication a problem? Was sex becoming stale or too infrequent?

Armed with the answers to these questions and with the help of a professional marriage counsellor, it is possible for a couple to get even closer than before the infidelity especially if this was in fact a cry for help. Men often stray during a wife's pregnancy for instance, or during the first few months after childbirth. Such men tell me that they feel pushed out by their wife's understandable preoccupation with the baby. Here's a classic case of communication breakdown. If men and women could talk about these pitfalls before becoming parents, and preferably before getting married, so much could be avoided. Rather than go out and find another bed partner, deal with what's causing your restlessness or discontentment.

Maybe the problem can be fixed relatively easily whereas infidelity will leave irreparable scars no matter what the outcome. Casual sex with another woman is hurtful enough but if you fall in love with someone else you will be caught in an emotional dilemma of frightening proportions, from which you may never come back. It may cost you your family and when you have children that price could be higher than you're prepared to pay.

In summary:
- think one hundred times before plunging into extra-marital sex
- if you do it, either keep it to one occasion or come clean about it
- don't do anything that will put your family's emotional or physical health in danger

- if your partner's been unfaithful, weigh up the whole relationship rather than just focusing on this one act of betrayal — don't let your ego and pride blind you to all the good stuff that's worth keeping

Communication difficulties

We should never assume we know what someone else is thinking or attribute motives to them, no matter how close we might be. We each have a unique perspective on the world and an individual moral code. As a society, we all have certain rules and standards to follow but this should not preclude personal integrity and following your own instincts. In a relationship, this can bring about clashes and misunderstandings. That's why you should try to pick a partner whose values and beliefs match yours whilst at the same time you remain individuals. I've always believed in the saying, 'Love isn't two people looking into each other's eyes; it's two people looking in the same direction.'

If you or your partner have not cleared the past and connected with the subconscious vibrations that govern your life it's very easy to get an entirely incorrect picture of what you are giving out to and receiving from your wife or girlfriend. You may feel attacked, criticised, judged, put down or rejected when these things were not intended at all. Conversely, you may be accused of giving offence when that was the last thing on your mind, simply because you are giving forth signals that you're unaware of. Everything that's been said in the book so far is designed to help you to build up this awareness so that when you make relationship mistakes in the future (and you will, just because you're human!) you'll accept them for what they are, learn from them and move on. Misunderstandings cause a good deal of stress and strain in a relationship as no-one likes to be unfairly accused.

The way we deliver a complaint is also crucial and that's where assertiveness skills come in. Fighting, disagreeing, and quarreling are all part of the relating process but even these can be positive if conducted in the right spirit. A sense of humour helps as does talking about the disagreement after it's over and learning to let go. If you keep harping on about how the other person has let you down, eventually there are no good feelings left. A good rule: when in doubt, ask. Don't accuse, ask, and listen. If you don't understand or agree, say so but don't nag or bully. Your wife is your partner, not your child to be chastised or taught a lesson. Empower yourself and always make sure that all your interactions leave the other party with their own power as well.

We have already seen how effective communication enhances a relationship and damages one when it's poorly managed. It is in my mind the single most important tool in stress reduction, in and out of marriage.

Children and parenting

It's pretty easy to see why children create a good deal of stress in a marriage. Right from when they are born, they intrude on the fabric of the marriage by shifting the group dynamics. As mentioned in the last section, fathers often resent the arrival of a child, especially the first, even when it's planned and wanted.

Although we are individuals, we are affected by the life-events of those around us. That's why we can't separate work stress from home stress and vice-versa. In a relationship as close as marriage it's very difficult to totally detach ourselves from what our partners are going through and feeling. That's why having good boundaries is so vital. However, an event like the arrival of a child and the pregnancy that precedes it cannot help but impinge on both partners.

Nowadays, men are encouraged to take a more and more active role in parenting (and of course many of you are doing it alone). I see this development as extremely positive. I'm noticing it everywhere and of course, writing this book has alerted me further to the ever-increasing presence of active male parents in our society.

It would've been unheard of even as recently as five years ago to see men out and about with children in their sole care. I saw a lovely sight a few months ago — a young average-looking guy bottle-feeding a baby by himself, leaning up against a wall in a park on a Saturday afternoon. How dare anyone suggest that the woman is the superior parent? Our fathers and grandparents simply grew up in an era that dictated men should go out and work and women should be the exclusive child-rearers. That day is gone and we are proving daily that parenting is more than genetics or biology. Even gay men are choosing to father or adopt children and are building successful families. Love is the only prerequisite for good parenting; however, it is not the only requirement.

Why is parenting stressful?

- the inherent responsibility it brings with it
- the changes in the relationship between parents
- the financial burdens and sacrifices involved in bringing up a child to adulthood
- having to understand all the developmental stages of a child, from baby to teenage to adult

Parenting begins right from pregnancy and childbirth. As much as a father looks forward to the birth of his child it can never be exactly the experience a mother has, either physically or emotionally. Pregnancy puts a good deal of strain on a marriage as well as bringing joy. A woman often feels less attractive and this can affect the couple's sex life; she may also be more moody, sensitive and tired than usual due to hormonal changes and this requires a lot of patience from her husband; routines are interrupted, social life has to be adjusted and there are all sorts of expensive preparations to be made.

Then the baby arrives and the husband feels redundant, as if his part in the proceedings happened nine months ago and he's no longer needed. I've heard many men, and some women, say that their marriage never felt the same, never recovered after the birth of the first child. Enlightened couples talk this over beforehand, discuss the inevitable changes a baby will bring to their lives and plan together how to handle them. Rearing children is no longer just a woman's domain; therefore a man and woman should discuss each one's role and how best to minimise stress.

Male clients often tell me that they feel almost like strangers in their own homes after the arrival of a newborn. The mother understandably focuses on the baby and has little time for extras like talking or making love. Sleep becomes a precious commodity and the whole household is disrupted, meals are probably patchy and the washing piles up. In time, the chaos reduces but the first few months are a nightmare, even when there is teamwork and understanding, let alone when there's not.

Sex can become a very sensitive issue. If a man has had to go without love-making for a few weeks at the tail-end of the nine-month pregnancy and now he has to cope with a fatigued, sleep-deprived, maybe irritable and non-horny wife, his patience is stretched to the limit. If a couple can stay close during this difficult time, they will weather the storm and one day the sun will appear again and they can laugh about the whole episode. A woman goes off sex after childbirth for very sound biological reasons, such as hormonal changes and fatigue, but also for psychological reasons. A new mother has to put so much energy into her baby, she has little left at the end of the day; she also transfers a lot of her tactile needs to the child who requires handling, feeding and touching all day long. She might suffer from post-natal depression, a condition that causes feelings of anxiety, extreme fatigue and 'the blues'. This can vary from mild to extreme depending on the individual and has to be monitored carefully.

Even when sex resumes, the parents of a young baby are continually at that child's beck and call and love-making is often interrupted or impossible to achieve. In fact, loss of privacy is one of the sacrifices of parenting right up till kids are old enough to leave home: babies cry, small children fight and teenagers barge in when they want something. Training them to respect your privacy as they expect their own to be helps but in a family, quiet solitude is still a rare commodity.

In unusual cases, I have been told by clients that, as children, they were the ones who felt excluded, that their parents were terribly in love and involved with each other to a point where their offspring felt unwanted. On further investigation I have found that parents like these did not particularly want children but ended up having one or two without being willing to adjust their relationship. Today, couples are quite consciously choosing to stay as a twosome. This seems preferable to having unwanted children or giving up careers and then resenting the family.

Children are stressful just by being who they are. Despite the joy they bring, they're demanding, ever-present, costly and often noisy, but remember that they didn't choose to be born. If you brought them here by choice or otherwise, you have an obligation to give them everything they need, including time, attention, reassurance, encouragement and support, not to mention love. Studies in recent decades show that these are just as vital to a child's development as food, shelter and material security. Freud said that money doesn't make us happy because it isn't a primal need whereas feeling loved and wanted are.

There is more education these days about what constitutes good parenting but there are also more stresses in general on parents, especially in the areas of the financial burdens of child-rearing, high unemployment for school-leavers, teenage drug problems and violence in our society.

It is not within the scope of this book to look into each of these areas although they most certainly cause stress. There are many books on the market that cover these topics in more detail including those I have listed in my bibliography.

With kids just remember:

- Emphasise the positive.
- Give them heaps of unconditional love.
- Keep the lines of communication open.
- Spend quality time with them.
- Demonstrate your love with lots of hugs and kisses, even when they're older and despite their protests.
- Respect their individuality.
- Keep rules to a minimum but enforce the ones you have.
- Don't try to make them carbon copies of yourself or pressure them into roles that you want for them.
- Let them find their own way but guide them and advise if you're asked.
- Most of all, trust and support them.

It's a tall order, being a parent, and I can testify that many fail at the job because I, as a counsellor, get to pick up the broken pieces, ten, twenty, thirty or forty years down the track. Just do your best and your kids will forgive you the rest.

Money

Money can cause stress in many ways as we shall see in the chapter on work, but within marriage, it has its most difficult and potentially destructive expression. They say that more marriages break up over problems related to money than for any other single reason but I still think that poor communication is at the root of most marriage failure because any problem, even one involving money, can be ironed out if two people can talk about it calmly and constructively. (Read about money in detail in Chapter 9.)

Having looked at all the pitfalls of marriage and some of the most common stress problems, is it still worth taking the risk? Consider that it is the ultimate personal commitment and when it works, you can know depths of joy not found in other relationships but because of the element of closeness in marriage, it can test human endurance and stretch the limits of patience to breaking point. That's why so many couples give up and break up and why others stay in brutal, lonely and desperately unhappy relationships rather than finding alternatives.

As with everything in life you get out of it what you put in. If you want a happy and long-lasting marriage you can have it, but as a partner you must put the work into yourself then into the relationship itself, which is a third and separate entity from you and your wife. Like a garden it needs tending, feeding and care. If you neglect it or take it for granted you have yourself to blame when you end up with just weeds and dead flowers.

The chapter ends on a topic that may seem negative but, in fact, can be just the opposite — breaking up and coming out of a relationship.

BREAKING UP

I have a theory that men leave a marriage only when there's a ready alternative, namely, another lover waiting; women leave to be free and independent. A man will take his freedom outside the home as he needs it, not necessarily sexual freedom but time for his hobbies, mates, sport, work, whatever. In the traditional family a woman is tied more to the home base and the demands of her children so she's likely to subdue her own desires and needs. Once the children have left home, if the marriage has not been a happy one, women can start to feel restless and seek fulfilment outside. When this happens it often comes as a complete shock to the husband who has been perfectly happy with the arrangement and assumed it would continue. I remember a client once saying to me, 'I was married for eighteen years and had no reason to think I wouldn't be married forever.'

When this issue comes up in the counselling room the woman invariably denies that her husband had no warning, insisting that she had made known her complaints thousands of times over the years. Obviously women are not clear and assertive enough in voicing their grievances and men, perhaps you are too quick to dismiss this as 'nagging' and are guilty of paying insufficient attention to the requests for change or discussion.

The process
The breaking-up process is inevitably a painful one but it can be made less stressful by a loving and co-operative attitude. Unfortunately, if one partner wants to break up and the other doesn't there's usually a lot of animosity and bitterness.

When there are children involved, I believe there is little choice but to put aside ego and hurt feelings for their sake and to show a united front, even if it's an act. Children are always innocent victims and they should be considered first and foremost. It is absolutely unforgiveable for warring parents to use the children as weapons. The reason partners do this is that each is seeking power and what better tool than a loved object like a child? The partner who does not want to end the marriage feels helpless and wants to find a way to punish the other person.

As with death, a grieving process is necessary and one of the key stages is anger. Referring back to the section on anger in Chapter 4, however, you will recall that we each need to resolve our own anger and not dump it on someone else, no matter how much we think they deserve it. This takes emotional maturity without which we are like rudderless ships afloat on a stormy sea. Difficult painful times in our lives test us but can also make us stronger, depending on how we respond to them.

Once again, honesty and communication play vital roles. If you want to end a relationship, talk to your partner rather than sneaking around or making arrangements to leave without discussion. You may have to put up with a few emotional scenes but it'll be worth it. Men are by nature less devious than women so you generally front up and say you want out but we can all be cowards when faced with a daunting emotional confrontation.

Even a break-up should be handled together, especially if you have children who need to be reassured that you're divorcing each other but not them. Sometimes a trial separation is more appropriate but I do advise that clear terms are laid down to avoid misunderstandings and further rifts. You need to be clear on how long the separation will be, whether you see each other during this period and whether you are going to see other people. Marriage counselling is advisable before resumption of the relationship after a separation, and the decision to live together again should be mutual, not just one person's choice.

If all attempts at reconciliation fail and a break-up is inevitable, there must be time and space allowed for both emotional and practical resolution — who lives where, division of property, arrangements for children, selling of assets, future of the relationship and so on. It's much easier to settle all this in a calm and rational atmosphere than as screaming enemies. If you're thinking it's easy to say and hard to do, consider that it's worth it in the long run because you have to live with yourself after the shouting dies down and you still have to relate to your wife if there are children. I remember someone once saying to me, 'When you have children, you never really break up.' Child custody arrangements are a source of great stress to many men who feel that family law is inequitable and discriminates against men. During any reform process, if enough people protest and have genuine causes for grievance, future generations may see a fairer arrangement. Children should go to whichever parent is best able to take care of them, regardless of gender, and the other parent should have reasonable access that does not disrupt the children's lives too much or that of the custodial parent. The details have to be ruled in court if the parents themselves cannot make an amicable settlement and that's why I stress the importance of ironing out your differences before you physically separate or get into divorce proceedings.

Breaking up over a third party is always a mistake: it leaves a bad taste in the mouth of the other partner, it creates a tremendous amount of bitterness and it's not healthy to break up over a new lover. If you have problems in your marriage, either sort them out between you and carry on or break up cleanly before seeking new partners. I strongly advise this as I have seen the pain caused by the type of infidelity that leads to divorce, when the unfaithful partner moves in with someone else or remarries. These rifts are almost impossible to heal and affect the future functioning of the broken family.

In the best of all possible worlds married couples would stay together and work out their troubles but there is no point in two people staying together if they make each other miserable. It's not 'failure' to give up on a relationship as long as you give it an honest try and do the right thing in breaking up. Sometimes, it takes more courage to go than to stay if you recognise you've made a mistake; staying could cause more pain in the long term. While we're all afraid of change and starting fresh, breaking away from a negative or destructive relationship can be an extremely liberating and evolutionary experience.

Resolution

Okay, so it's all over and you find yourself single for the first time in years, perhaps many years. What to do?

See a counsellor or attend a group to resolve for yourself the reasons for the 'failed' relationship. By coming to terms with what happened, and especially your part in it, you can rid yourself of any unwanted 'garbage' and move confidently into the next association when the time is right. I don't ever recommend jumping straight into another affair as it will be either transitional or, worse still, you might make a premature commitment out of loneliness or a reactionary urge. Men usually find this advice less palatable than women because, as I've already said, men prefer not to be alone, especially in their living arrangements.

It's important to give yourself time to grieve, release and heal. Join a support group by all means but make sure it's not one of those that encourages self-pity and going over and over the past. When you're ready, get out and mix with men *and* women to get your confidence back, take your time, enjoy being single and grab the opportunity to learn more about yourself. As and when it's appropriate, I strongly recommend having 'closure' with your partner.

Closure involves 'closing' off the relationship in a way that brings dignity and respect to both parties. The best way is to meet on neutral ground after everything is settled. Wish each other well, parting with a hug and forgiving whatever has caused the break-up. Unfortunately, it's usually the case that one partner is willing and the other not for a variety of reasons. It's a healthy and beautiful way to end a partnership but if it's not possible you can still do it on your own with your thoughts, a meditation or, best of all, in writing. Here's a suggestion for a closure letter — it involves four sets of goodbyes to be said: to the things you liked about the relationship, to the things you didn't like, to the dreams you had for the relationship and finally to the person you have had the break-up with. You can choose whether or not to mail this letter after it's written. The effect will be the same whether you send it or not as the point is to let go in a loving way. If you have a lot of bitterness and anger to get out, write it all down but definitely don't mail a venomous letter — just burn it as a symbol of release.

If you feel like staying home by yourself for a while, do so as it's very healthy to grieve and cry if it's necessary. Playing the macho man is not going to help you feel better except in the short term. Sooner or later you have to face your own thoughts in the solitude of your bedroom when you will experience the 'dark night of the soul', the loneliest place there is. But if you find yourself there you may finally realise you are never alone.

Out of pain comes gain. This a cliché but it is also true. Live your life hopefully, for without that you may as well not bother to get up in the morning. If things go wrong despite your best efforts, don't waste your energy in regret. See everything as a learning experience, and if you can, believe that it's all for an unknown purpose. I used to be a fighter till I realised that the only thing I was fighting was myself. Be your own best friend; then everything else is a bonus.

If you are still in a relationship or about to enter a serious one, I have written a partnership agreement to help you. You can use it as part of your wedding vows or keep it as a private pact between you. Sometimes it's good to have things written down; it makes them more real.

RELATIONSHIP AGREEMENT

I promise in this relationship to offer the following:
- gentleness, sensitivity and tact
- quality time to spend together every day
- consideration of your feelings
- personal freedom and autonomy
- acceptance of the way you do things
- total responsibility for my own feelings, desires, needs and choices
- consulting you on plans and arrangements that affect you
- honest discussion of problems and differences
- speaking up about my grievances

- allowing you to follow your own dreams.

I will minimise the following:

- attacks, criticism and suspicions
- dumping of my frustrations, anger, hang-ups, insecurities and stress
- projecting of my problems onto you
- referring to the past for ammunition and comparisons
- defensiveness
- resenting others who are close to you and being jealous or possessive
- judging how you think and feel
- moodiness, sulkiness
- arguing about differences and preferences
- expounding on things you may feel differently about
- expecting you to fulfil my needs or make me happy.

Positive self-talk

- I never use another as a scapegoat in a relationship, but identify and deal with my own issues.
- I am conscious of the need to maintain freshness and joy in relationships.
- I accept and respect difference.
- I do not play guilt games.
- I live my life hopefully, no matter what.

Chapter 8

SEXUALITY

In some ways, this is the most important chapter of the book, not because you guys are supposed to rank sex as the best thing in life but because I have always believed that it is in the sexual arena that men experience the most potential and real stress. So far in this book I have tried to point out that, beyond genetics, you males are conditioned to behave in particular ways. Do you all really love football and beer above everything else, or did you learn to feel that way because your father and grandfather did or you picked up these habits from school and friends? There's nothing wrong with football and beer — addiction to alcohol is another matter — enjoying a few beers while watching sport is almost synonomous with the male sex all over the world. It just irks me to see men playing out the 'yobbo' role so convincingly as if it's the expected thing when I believe you want as much diversity and variety as women do. Those of you who are not into stereotypical male pleasures can sometimes be found at the other end of the spectrum — the yuppie executive with his mobile phone, briefcase and immaculate suit, a heart attack waiting to happen. Yuppie or yobbo? What a choice of set styles!

What has this to do with sex? Well, there are more sexual stereotypes than any other kind in our society — the bosomy female and the salivating male or the hunky athlete and the draped blonde bimbo. It's all around us, in our advertising, media, the news, business, consumer products. Sex sells — how many times have we been fed that line and of course it's true. While narrow-minded attitudes to sex are very damaging, men and women, but especially men, are put under enormous pressure to manifest society's perfect images and to perform on cue like trained monkeys.

In this chapter, I'm going to look at all aspects of human sexuality, how we as a society deal with sex and, hopefully, explode some common myths.

WHAT IS SEXUALITY?

If I asked the question of a bunch of you in the street, I bet your answers would involve intercourse, genitals and orgasm because these are the three things that most people believe make up human sexuality. In fact, sexuality has nothing specifically to do with these things. They are only the outward expression of sexuality.

Every one of us is born sexual and we remain sexual till the day we die even if we have never once had intercourse. Sexual energy comes from the life-force and is contained within us, tied to our creativity, intuition and inner essence. So we are sexual twenty-four hours a day, whether we are making a speech, washing dishes or driving a car. It has nothing to do with sexy thoughts or actions or behaviour. Some people exude their sexuality more than others because they're more conscious of it and they've brought it up to the surface — have you noticed how your sexual aura increases when you are first in love and having a lot more sex than usual?

Once you realise this power is always within you, you need never feel deprived again. When you're actively having sex it's fine, and when you're not it's still fine. The key is to release sexual energy every day and not to let it get blocked. Repression is very harmful to both body and soul. Any effort to keep sexual energy locked away never works — it will simply come out in another darker form, as we have seen with the recent revelations of religious child-carers who have abused and violated their charges.

Releasing sexual energy

We can release sexual energy in several ways:

- sexual activity with another
- self-pleasuring/masturbation
- rechannelling sexual energy
- celibacy/spiritual enlightenment

The last one is not as difficult as it sounds; living a life without sex does not have to be a life of lack and longing as many of us would imagine. Not only nuns and priests and ascetics choose celibacy as a way of life. Many ordinary people are now doing so for emotional and/or health reasons. My aunt in America is a nun who has lived one of the most fulfilling, interesting and full lives of anyone I know because she channelled her 'sexual' energy into her work, her students, travel, counselling and, of course, her religious faith. The body is governed by the mind and a mind filled with interesting and fulfilling thoughts and ideas has no time to feel deprived. Those of you who believe that you must have sex (meaning orgasm) every day are fooling yourselves and creating undue stress, especially if you are single and don't have a regular sex partner. I hear this all the time and it is one of the great sexual myths. If you feel the need to masturbate or have sexual intercourse every day, and sometimes several times a day, you are probably bored out of your mind or using sex for the wrong reasons. Before you slam this book shut in protest, hear me out. I want to talk now about sex addiction.

Sex addiction

As with other forms of addiction, we become hooked on sex to the point where we hand over our power to it and we feel complete only when we're doing it. The need grows stronger and greater until it virtually takes over our lives. Everything else is subjugated to it. In severe forms it can be just as harmful as drug addiction, for sex becomes a drug that must be taken at regular intervals. This is just a mind game but the more you feed your body what it believes it needs, the more real the need becomes, as with chemical addiction. The chemicals that are released during sex give us a type of 'high' and it's highly addictive under the right conditions, as with new lovers, depressed or anxious subjects and the very young.

If you recognise that you have an addiction problem, firstly acknowledge it and get help if you think it's pretty severe; next, begin to fill your life with other satisfying things so that you're not looking to sex to give you everything you need. Channelling your sexual energies into creative pursuits, hobbies, a variety of interests, stretching your mind and imagination, love of nature, animals, children, enjoyable work, art, music — the possibilities are endless — is the best strategy. Even if you have a sexual partner, this new attitude will take the pressure off her and allow sex between you to evolve to its own rhythm, and to happen naturally as it should.

As we saw in Chapter 7, a lot of stress around marital sex is caused by differences in sexual interest and pressure from one partner on the other. Finding other ways to be intimate is really important: holding hands in front of TV, taking walks together, listening to music, occasional nights out or romantic dinners in, mutual non-sexual massage, stroking each other in bed in place of intercourse, and so on. Male sexuality is expressed differently from female, for the simple reason that the former is overt while the latter is hidden and more subtle. A woman can express love in non-sexual ways much more easily for this reason. I remember watching a video about Tantric sex with a mixed group of mine. It was pretty explicit and I called for responses afterwards. Our resident cynic, a Scottish woman, said bluntly, 'How many men do you know who would be willing to try that?' We all laughed but she was right — men show a strong resistance to anything that may take away from the idea of virility. Tenderness and softness is all right in its place but it can't compare to a good old-fashioned roll in the hay; taking a woman strongly in the missionary or doggie position is still hard to beat.

What if I were to tell you that you can actually improve your sexual performance, remove a lot of the inherent anxiety that goes with being a male in bed and have a great time physically, would you change your mind?

Spiritual sex

Believe it or not, sex can be a very spiritual experience. Sex begins in the mind — initially it's the idea of sex that gets us horny, that makes a woman wet and a man hard. The physical act is the result of this and too many men turn it into the be-all and end-all. It's great but it's limited, especially if it's over too soon, and it usually is if only the physical side is emphasised. It's a catch-22 situation but it doesn't have to be.

Spiritual sex is also sometimes called 'sacred' sex and comes from the Eastern philosophies of Tantra which combined sexuality with mysticism and religion. It is not necessary to follow these beliefs slavishly in order to enhance your sex life but it is valuable to incorporate some of its tenets into your usual love-making practices, in other words, expand your repertoire, shift your thinking, get creative. These are some of the ideas I have personally found very enhancing:

- Shift the emphasis from genitals to an all-body approach.
- Make love at a much slower, gentler pace.
- Aim to connect at every level, not just the physical.
- Go to bed to get horny rather than because you're horny.
- Incorporate a lot more touch into love-making and sometimes engage in non-sexual massage in place of sex.
- Take turns nurturing each other in bed so that you don't always have to assume the dominant, strong position.
- Experiment and have fun.
- Keep your love-making place, usually bed, as a sacred space, kept only for positive interaction — never fight or argue or discuss problems there.

These are all positive and practical suggestions that I have 'Westernised' for the purpose of clarity and simplicity. If you try these ideas with a willing partner you will find your sex life improving beyond the sexual arena. Your communication will be more relaxed, your love-making more tactile and sensual, your relationship in general more deep and intimate. Your wife or girlfriend will thank you as women usually complain to me that men are too quick, too eager and too physical. There's a time for raunchy intercourse but, as you care more for a woman, it's nice to slow down and enjoy other dimensions, explore each other's bodies and try new things in bed.

Sexual attitudes

From what I've said so far you have probably garnered some general information about the way our society views sex, even in the so-called enlightened nineties. Our attitudes are very much based on the Victorian moral ethic which is rooted in patriarchal standards and steeped in guilt. That's why our school sex education systems are so poor and why teenage girls are still getting pregnant and why we now have something called AIDS.

As a society — and by this I mean Western society in general — we are afraid of our own sexuality. This applies more to women than men because of the way we've all been conditioned, but men too are often hooked on old-fashioned ideas about what sex should be and their role in it. I had one guy ring me up on my sex advice radio show to ask me about his fetish, which he was very embarrassed to reveal. I was dreading what was going to come out but it was only unusual — he gets turned on by women in hair-rollers! He was perceptibly relieved when I told him there was nothing wrong with this. He was just one of a huge number of callers who rang to enquire about their desires and preferences, anxious to find out if it's okay, if they're 'normal'. I say anything goes in the bedroom as long as it doesn't hurt you or your partner and doesn't involve powerless participants such as animals and children.

There's also an amazing degree of ignorance about sex, health, disease and anatomy. A guy once asked me if he could catch his wife's cervical cancer from having sex with her. He was totally serious and was reluctant to believe me when I told him it was impossible.

Sex shouldn't be a mindless act; it should lift us to a higher plane that transcends our daily existence. Instead it has been debased and abused more than almost anything else in our society. Because it sells it is seen by many as a commodity to be bought and sold for the best price. Mind you, having said that, I think prostitution is one of the most honest games in town as it's a straight transaction — a service for a fee. Many other forms of selling in our community are far more dirty. Perhaps it helps to distinguish 'public' sex from private. A quickie in a brothel or with a one-night stand should not be regarded in the same light as love-making with a partner you care for. The latter deserves your tenderness and all the finesse you can muster; otherwise, as we saw before, it can cause major stress in your life.

Fantasy

Men are renowned for the love of sexual fantasy, erotic literature and pornography. These are all good and can enhance love-making considerably. A client of mine loved to go to a pub with his mates on Friday nights and watch strippers. He said his wife absolutely hated this and wouldn't let him make love to her when he came home because she said he was turned on by the strippers and not by her. So what? Anything can turn us on — that's the point I've been trying to make about limited attitudes towards sexuality. It is limitless and expansive if we allow it to be. We can feel sexual about a thousand people in our lifetimes — it doesn't mean we want to actually have sex with them, and even if we do it doesn't matter if we don't act on it. Even apart from commitments we may have to a relationship, having lots of casual encounters is unhealthy for the body, mind and soul. I say this from a psychological rather than moral standpoint.

Many things can stimulate you sexually — the wind on your face, a delicious meal, a successful business deal, a piece of beautiful music, a sunset, the hug of a beloved friend. Remember I'm speaking of sexuality in the wider sense, linked to creativity, spirituality and the life-force. From this angle, we can be intimate on a number of levels with many, many people and even animals or inanimate things. What could be more sensual than stroking a cat's fur or running your hand along a fine piece of wood or touching rain? Expand your thinking on this subject — I know you won't be sorry. The other aspect of fantasy is not to feel guilt, no matter what your fantasy is. Only you own the contents of your mind and nothing is wrong as long as you leave it in the realms of fiction. Some men try to live out their fantasy and by doing so, kill it. Fantasy can only exist in the mind; that is its nature. By acting on it, you take it from a mind-game to reality and either get into trouble because what you want to do is illegal or you lose the thrill of the unattainable dream. So many men and women rang me on precisely this topic during the two years my show was on air. One guy told me that he pestered his girlfriend for months to live out his (very common) fantasy of a threesome with another woman. Against her better judgement, she agreed, and found that she enjoyed it so much, she wanted to try it again, this time with another bloke! This was an outome my caller hadn't expected and he phoned me to say he couldn't cope with the idea of sharing his girlfrind with another guy. He didn't realise this till he was put to the test, and now he regretted bitterly having asked his girlfriend to play out his fantasy in the first place. It's a case of not wishing too hard for what you want because you might get it!

My rule about threesomes is to be clear on why you're doing it; choose the other participants carefully and never involve people you're emotionally attached to. I've seen this particular sexual experiment go horribly wrong and break up relationships because the parties weren't clear on what they were buying into before they jumped in.

Other common fantasies are rape, playing with school-girls, nurse/patient, French maid, discipline of various kinds, being in a brothel, being caned by a teacher and so on. Then of course there are wild and fantastic fantasies that are limited only by the scope of the imagination of the individual.

Using fantasy in bed to enhance sex life is a controversial area. I see no harm in a man making love to his wife whilst thinking of Sharon Stone — his partner could very well be thinking of John Travolta at the same time! It would, however, worry me if he were imagining that he was making love to a woman at work or someone else he actually knew, especially if it was a recurring thing.

Sex aids are also part of the fantasy package. They're great as long as they stay aids and don't become the main event. A vibrator, 'blue' movie or strap-on dildo adds an element of fun and fantasy to love-making as do dressing up, mild S&M and role-playing in bed. As long as both partners are willing it can only add to a couple's sex life. But when does fantasy cross over to something darker?

DEVIANCE

This term covers a lot of ground as, sociologically, it encompasses any activity that is not considered to be the 'norm' by the society judging it. Therefore in Australia, for instance, prostitution, homosexuality and pornography are all classified as deviance, together with paedophilia, B&D, S&M, rape, obscene phone calls, indecent exposure, bestiality, sodomy and unusual sexual practices. In my last book, *Sex — everything you want to know and why*, I cover these in detail, but for the purposes of a men's stress book I guess these are relevant only if you happen to be engaging in any of these practices and it's causing you stress! If it is causing you stress, it's tied up with guilt and the fear of being caught. I think the best way for me to cover this topic is to illustrate with a few case studies.

One client was a 'peeping Tom' despite the fact that he was happily married with a child. He said the urge was so great at times that he would rush out of the house without any warning and find the nearest window that he could look into. He had been caught and warned off but the danger only added to the excitement. It was pretty obvious from our discussions that it wasn't the sight of a woman undressing that turned him on; it was the risks he was taking and the guilt that ensued.

We had to uncover the root of these feelings and urges, which we did. It turned out that when he was a boy his family lived in an old house with a lane running behind it. An old neighbour used to throw his magazines out for rubbish collection in this laneway. My client rummaged through one day and found pornographic material which naturally excited him. He began sneaking out as often as he could to read these books but he lived in mortal terror of being caught by his parents. The sexual arousal and the fear–danger became associated in his young mind and, as an adult, he felt strong urges to go out and repeat these illicit pleasures although he couldn't understand why. It just happened to take the form of peeping but it could just as easily have been obscene phone calls or 'flashing' to achieve the same effect.

Another client was only twenty-four and handsome with a great job and lovely girlfriend. He became addicted to pornography to the point where it had him totally in its grip. He reported that he could think of little else and nearly lost his job because he kept running out of work in the middle of the day to go to sex shops and look at magazines and pictures. The reason in his case was linked to a very religious and stern father who had died a short while before my client's addiction began. Bereavement takes on many strange and subtle forms and, in this case, the young man could not come to grips with his father's death as they had never been close and he 'broke out' in his grief by doing the very thing his father would've hated the most. Backlash? Self-hatred? Anger at his father? All of the above? I don't know. All I know is that my clients are only set free from their demons when they understand their origins.

Another case involved a middle-aged man who liked to wear women's knickers. When his wife first found out his guilty secret, she threatened to leave him but he agreed to seek counselling to find out the reason for his unusual habit. The answer was simple — remember how logical the subsconscious mind is; it basically delivers what you ask for. As a boy, my client used to be allowed to join in his mother's afternoon tea parties with the ladies. As children often do he would lie on the floor in the middle of the gathering and he found that he could see right up the skirts of the women. This excited him although he didn't know why at the time and it stuck in his mind that frilly, satiny female underwear was a turn-on. In his adult life, this fantasy was translated into the wearing of these garments. Bear in mind that we're not speaking here of perverts or weirdos, but ordinary decent guys who are just as puzzled about their odd tastes and behaviour as other people are.

Cross-dressing

There's a lot of misunderstanding about this practice. Although some men who enjoy it do get sexually aroused, there are other reasons for it. It has nothing to do with homosexuality or sex change. It is simply the need some men feel for being in women's clothing. Some say it makes them feel good, others feel they were born into the wrong sex but they don't want to change over to women completely and yet others enjoy the sensuality of female apparel. With some guys it's only a particular piece of clothing like underwear or dresses; others go the whole hog and take on an entire female persona, even changing their personalities to match. Married men who are into cross-dressing need very understanding wives and lovers, some of whom participate in the practice with their partners and even engage in sexual activities while their men are dressed up. This is an entirely personal choice. At the other end of the spectrum, there are women who find the whole idea abhorrent and break up the relationship over it.

As always, I find the underlying reasons far more compelling than the external behaviour. Many cross-dressers I've counselled come from childhoods where their spontaneity and sense of fun were tightly reined in by dominating mothers, and very strict religious backgrounds where rules and rigid standards were more important than love and freedom. With this predominant influence, kids grow up to be afraid of their own impulses and they learn to repress them. Cross-dressing is an outlet for some of these men as they can release their inhibitions within a role, wearing a 'costume'. I've noticed that these particular transvestites exhibit almost spilt personalities, often becoming loud, flamboyant, outrageous and extremely extrovert as a woman, and reverting to shy, quiet, introverted men when the women's gear comes off.

Referring back to the subject of polarities earlier in the book, this form of outlet becomes unnecessary when there is no guilt about behaviour and a man can be totally himself in all aspects. Guilt plays a large part in cross-dressing and all the other aberrations I've mentioned in this section. Without guilt, a lot of the 'kick' is removed and the deviant behaviour ceases to be as pleasurable. As long as we are in reactionary mode, fighting off our past influences and desperately trying not to be our parents, we are likely to keep feeling ashamed of our deepest feelings, thoughts and desires. These must find manifestation and thus we have the addictions, aggression, grief, violence, relationship failure, suicide and heartbreak that saturate our society and our consciousness. The behaviours we act out are merely the physical manifestations of our pain. No-one who is happy hurts an animal or child, commits a crime or kills someone. Concentrate on your own peace and truth and whatever is troubling you will take care of itself. Of course, you only have a problem with a so-called deviance if it's bothering you. If you're enjoying it at a moderate level and you're not hurting anyone else you are certainly entitled to continue it, and don't let anyone tell you it's 'wrong' because we each have our own moral code; truth and ethics can never be absolutes.

When clients walk in and start telling me their problems, I listen patiently but then I tell them to forget all about them as the only thing we can fix is ourselves. It is so tempting to say our troubles are caused by our society or our partners or lack of money or a horrible boss; that's just a cop-out. There is no reality you haven't created yourself. Own it and admit your darkest desires and meanest thoughts. You will free your life.

SEX EDUCATION

Sex is an area in which few of us experience much freedom. It is rife with hang-ups and insecurities which cancel much of the joy that is our birthright. Think about how you learnt about sex. It's unlikely that your parents talked to you about it frankly or in detail. Your questions at home were probably glossed over or maybe you even got a slap for daring to ask about such things. Most of what you found out came from the schoolyard, locker room, mates and experimentation in the back seats of cars. School programmes are woefully inadequate and at any rate should not be expected to replace home tuition. The family is where children should learn about sex so that they understand from an early age how natural it is. There does not need to be a fuss made — kids' questions should just be dealt with honestly as they come up. Modern parents are much more confident in this area and there's a lot more help these days in the form of reading material and educational information. As with so many other things, attitudes to sex are passed down from one generation to another and can affect a child's whole future. If a boy hears his father speak of women as sex objects, this will colour his own behaviour towards his girlfriends and lovers as he grows up.

General sexual attitudes in the home have a lasting effect on the members of the family. For instance, if Mum and Dad show no affection to each other, children believe that's the way married couples should act; if sex is not talked about openly and is considered a taboo subject, that stays in a young person's mind long after they leave home; unrealistic and overly strict ideas about morality put fear, guilt and repression into impressionable imaginations. If a parent comes across a child masturbating and reacts negatively, this immediately creates shame and makes the child feel 'dirty'; it also follows that the desire to masturbate and the accompanying pleasure must also be 'bad' when, in fact, it is totally natural for a child to explore his own body and find pleasure in it. This is biology, not carnal lust!

I remember a guy ringing me on the radio show about his little boy of only eighteen months who loved to rub himself against his teddy bear as if having sex with it. My caller was horrified and didn't know if he should stop him. I explained that the baby wasn't having a sexual experience but rather a tactile one. It felt nice and comforting to rub his penis onto a favourite toy and it was all part of natural exploration. It would die off as the child grew interested in other things around him.

Why is it that sex is the only sin people seem to be ashamed of, even when they've done nothing wrong? It's because churches have always focused on it and most of us grew up with the message that hell-fire was licking at our heels if we experienced one moment of sexual pleasure, touched ourselves or experimented with another person. When I think of the ignorance my generation grew up with I can hardly believe it — I used to think that B&D stood for Black and Decker and STDs had something to do with long-distance phone calls! Most of the world's unhappiness can be laid squarely at the door of bigoted and overly proscriptive attitudes. The guilt that is absorbed in childhood affects everything we do in our sexual lives and, in turn, our relationships. A friend of mind coined a very true phrase — 'to many people, the root of all evil is the root!' For me, this quote from Freda Warrington's novel, A *dance in blood velvet* sums up my preferred philosophy about sex: 'Sex even in all its animal, feverish urgency, was not a sin but an offering to Heaven.'

We shall now see how much of what I've been saying also affects the way we perform sexually.

SEXUAL DYSFUNCTION

For men, the two key problems relating to sexual dysfunction are impotence and premature ejaculation. I have worked extensively with clients suffering these conditions but I don't propose to go into detailed descriptions of them here. You know what they mean and, if you're an average guy, you would've experienced both of them at some point in your life. They're far more common than men would like to admit and women realise.

There are basically three reasons for them happening — hormonal, physical, emotional. A blood test will ascertain if it's the first one, and for the second possibility consult your doctor who can run various tests and recommend drug therapy or physical aids.

Only after you have eliminated these two likely reasons should you look at psychological causes. These are the hardest to work out and you don't want to put yourself through an emotional investigation unless it is needed.

When clients come to me they have usually been checked out hormonally and physically so I then need to find out what could be causing the guy stress and/or anxiety, the two direct causes of sexual dysfunction.

Too many men allow sexual problems to continue without seeking help, either because of misguided pride or the belief that the condition will right itself. It generally doesn't for the simple reason that, whilst the problem itself might have been temporary, it will usually go on because of the inherent anxiety that attaches itself to the sufferer. So the condition is self-generating and multiplies instead of decreasing.

Be clear that I am not speaking here of an occasional inability to achieve or maintain erection or reaching orgasm too quickly once or twice. In psychology, behaviour is only significant if it forms a recurring pattern; one-off events don't count as they may be an aberration. You fellas don't like it even if it happens only once but please don't worry or think about it unduly as you might create a problem where none exists. However, if it starts to happen on a regular basis, don't put up with it — get help! Very often, the condition was triggered by a specific stress event so it really helps if you can identify one. As a check for yourself, try to trace back to any stress event that might have occurred in the last few monts.

You are not a machine — the things that happen to you emotionally directly affect the functioning of your body as we saw in Chapter 1. The more you try to be the tough macho man, the more likely that performance breakdown will happen.

You might be interested to learn that during the years I have worked with male sexual dysfunction I have found a direct correlation between these problems and being the first child in the family. Remember I earlier profiled the first child as being perfectionist, controlling, rigid, dutiful and hard-working. Well, they sometimes approach sex in the same way, as something to be done perfectly and conscientiously rather than as a natural process that should flow with feelings, touch and spiritual ease. Years of this can wear the body, mind and soul down until one day the body rebels and says — I don't want to do this any more!

Sexual dysfunctions are largely a product of the mind except in specific cases where a physical problem, a drug or a chronic condition causes them. 'Performance anxiety' is a key trigger for both impotence and premature ejaculation. Men are expected to be permanent studs, ever-ready to get hard and get into action. This might be fine when you're twenty and think of nothing but sex. When you get older and begin to have other responsibilities and dare I say it — stress! — sexual prowess can be adversely affected. Libido too can decrease as can general interest. If you take my advice and de-focus intercourse and physical performance, you will end up having a better time in bed overall.

Unfortunately, society puts a great deal of pressure on male sexuality and a man who's less than perfect every time he makes love is made to feel inadequate. That's why it's so important for you not to identify with any aspect of yourself as being the only one. You are no less valuable whether you're having successful sex or not. This is a very sensitive area and I daresay many of you are thinking that as a woman I couldn't possibly understand, but I have been a lover of men and although my partners did not suffer a chronic sexual dysfunction, there are always fluctuations in sexual interest and performance that affect a couple's interactions. Also, my clients have shared very openly and honestly with me their fears and insecurities in this area. In every case, the big issue is that of feeling 'like a man'. I say again nothing outside you can ever be responsible for who you are or what you feel; it always comes from within.

On a more practical note, an event or situation in your life can put you off sex. One common reason is a broken relationship. Many chaps report impotence after a divorce or during a separation, especially where they are the unwilling partners. Obviously it has to do with rejection and bruised egos and feeling vulnerable. Sex opens us up emotionally in a way that nothing else does and it's perfectly natural to close off when you've been very badly hurt. This is strictly a temporary state unless you worry yourself into prolonging the condition.

Some guys give up trying altogether, stop dating and stay alone; others keep trying, endure more 'failures' and increase anxiety to the point where they can't perform at all. Time, self-love and an understanding partner are the best cures in these cases. Criticising and doubting yourself is the worst thing you can do.

We need to distinguish between impotence and premature ejaculation. Impotence is simply the inability to achieve or maintain erection. This can be brought on by deep-seated anxiety or simple things such as fatigue, distraction and stress. Occasional bouts should be left alone, chronic occurrence should be referred to a doctor initially and then a counsellor, if necessary. There are many cures and aids available these days and counselling can help to identify the cause and minimise the anxiety factors.

Premature ejaculation, or PE as it's commonly known, is a bit more complex because it is less temporary and more deeply rooted in the past and/or emotional issues. Recall, if you would, the points I've raised about guilt and sex education. PE is a classic example of what happens when the negative effects of these two aspects of sexuality come together in a child or adolescent to cause pressure and problems.

Look at the nature of PE. It is, in simple terms, reaching climax too quickly, which of course is unsatisfying for the man and his partner. It is caused by a trigger reaction in the brain that is learned by repetitive behaviour. When a boy is first experimenting with sex, it is usually under hurried conditions — masturbating in the toilet or under the covers at night, playing with the girl next door behind the shed and, later, his first experience of sex in the back seat of a car or somewhere similar. The three key ingredients are urgency, danger and hurry. The first time for a male is often as uncertain and unsatisfying as it is for a female. The earlier a boy starts masturbating and the later he experiences actual intercourse, the more likely he is to suffer from PE as an adult for the simple reason that masturburtion is essentially a quick exercise whilst love-making brings in emotions, another person's feelings and slower responses. The brain learns habits very easily and after a few years of a certain set behaviour, the reaction is automatic. It takes a lot of time and patience to undo these patterns as we've seen throughout this book. Impotence can come and go overnight while PE tends to take longer to fix and can be chronic over many years. Some men and their partners just accept it as an inevitable part of their love-making when it doesn't have to be. Any good sex manual will outline exercises that will reduce the occurrence of PE until the brain eventually learns a new lesson. Other measures that help are — having more sex! It will please you guys to learn that more regular sex cuts back the speed of the trigger mechanism which brings on ejaculation. Spontaneous sex is more effective than planned sex so that the mind does not have time to build up anxiety or create the expectation of failure. Having sex with the woman on top helps a lot of sufferers as there's less movement lying underneath and therefore less likelihood of an early climax.

With all sexual dysfunction, nothing is as helpful as a relaxed attitude. Deep breathing is marvellous prior to going to bed and also any light and enjoyable exercise, a bit of reading or television — whatever makes you feel good. Try to put aside the stresses of the day by taking a bath, listening to a tape or doing a short meditation. The practices of sacred sex I mentioned earlier are particularly useful where sex is creating any pressure in your life or losing its pleasure and joy.

A sexual dysfunction that relates to women but affects you indirectly is being non-orgasmic. If you have a non-orgasmic partner, keep in mind that you are not responsible but of course if you love the person you will want her to enjoy love-making to the point of climax as you do. If she never can, encourage her to seek help from a professional sex therapist as there might be a reason from her past that can be sorted out. If she just finds it difficult to orgasm, work together as a couple to improve the ways in which you make love, and experiment till your partner can relax sufficiently to climax without difficulty. Don't get focused on intercourse as the only way to find satisfaction. I say the same thing to women who get frustrated with impotent partners or husbands who are PE sufferers. Mutual masturbation is exciting and stimulating, oral sex is a popular alternative and of course there are any number of sex aids on the market to help out when the real thing is unavailable.

ORAL SEX

I feel I should say something separately about oral sex as this form of love-making seems to cause a great deal of stress and conflict in relationships. The usual complaint from men is that their wives or girl-friends won't do it or don't like it. I have to admit that the women who really enjoy going down on a man are in the minority. Those who like it seem to really, really like it but the rest are either revolted by the idea or simply not interested. Men on the other hand nearly always love it and want it a lot. So there's a potential conflict straightaway. One female client told me her husband had sent her in to see me so that I could tell her she should give him oral sex! Another client was told by her husband that she had till the end of the year to perform oral sex on him or he was leaving the marriage! This kind of pressure is certainly not going to help the situation. No-one has the right to force a partner to do things sexually that they don't want to do.

My suggestion for oral sex is that it be used as part of the foreplay process rather than for ejaculation purposes because most women dislike the idea of a man climaxing in their mouths. If a woman loves you she probably enjoys every part of you including your penis and would have no problem kissing it. But don't insist on more if she really doesn't want it.

HOMOSEXUALITY

This book is being written for men in general and not any particular section of the male species but I want to make mention of the stress of being gay. If you are a gay man, you have stresses that are specific to your sexual preference. You are part of a sub-culture and that's always difficult. Your life style is open to scrutiny, misunderstanding and bigotry. Low self-esteem is rife amongst homosexuals and stress lowers the efficiency of the immune system so it's possible that gay men contract AIDS more readily for this reason. Such sexual practices as oral sex and anal intercourse are also high risk but I don't need to explain these facts in detail after the plethora of literature and information about AIDS we've all been exposed to in recent decades. Safe sex is obligatory for homosexuals and heterosexuals — that is just a fact of living in the 1990s and into the new century.

There are many arguments about why men and women are gay and many people in our society find the idea abhorrent, judging gays to be people of loose morals and promiscuous ways. As I've said throughout this book, morals are a private matter, not a collective issue. Everyone should look to their own behaviour and not judge others or attribute motives where there is lack of understanding. Anyway, this is not a book about ethics or right and wrong. I have to help real people with real problems in my line of work, and in this book my aim is to advise on the reduction of stress. So, if you are a gay man and you feel stressed about it, look to the reasons for this.

If it's social pressure or the fact of being in a minority, decide if your need to be gay is optional. If it's not, then you'll have to come to terms with the inherent difficulties of choosing an alternative life style. It means you will have to live your life with much more courage and integrity than others in order to withstand the 'slings and arrows' that are sure to come your way. Live by your own convictions and trust your instincts; don't let others put you down — how do you know what they do in their bedrooms! Treat your own body with respect as well as the lovers you come in contact with. In the next chapter, I will be looking at health issues so I'll leave it at that for now.

Keep in mind that based on my philosophy of human sexuality being a full-time thing, such labels as homosexuality, bi-sexuality and heterosexuality become irrelevant. We're just all sexual. How we choose to express that sexuality is our right to decide. If homosexuality is genetic as some theorists believe then there's no choice involved anyway.

ONE-NIGHT STANDS

I've spoken extensively about sex in marriage so I couldn't let this chapter close without a mention of the other end of the spectrum — casual sex. Sex can be casual in two ways — physically or emotionally. One-night stands are an obvious form of uncommitted encounter but even a long-term affair can be casual if deeper feelings aren't engaged.

Nowadays people are much more wary of having multiple partners due to health risks but it still goes on. All I suggest is that you never make an exception to the condom rule and keep casual exchanges away from risky areas such as oral sex or anal intercourse.

On the emotional front, be aware that an encounter that is casual for you may not be for the person you're having sex with, so be very clear about your intentions before anything happens. Never, never promise to get in touch again if you're definitely not interested. You may think you're being kind but brutal honesty can actually be kinder in the long run. Be honest and up-front right from the start. If it's very clearly a one-night stand to you, thank the woman in question after you have sex and say goodbye with respect and dignity. Acting like a pig is neither necessary nor very uplifting for either party.

Sex is one of our most beautiful and natural gifts. You can learn to be better at it as you mature but being relaxed about it is a good place to start. It's all right when you're seventeen to laugh about it, crack jokes and make fun of women but if you're still doing this at thirty or forty, you might want to ask yourself why. Just as a lot of women have difficulty in coming to terms with their sexual pleasure, some men can't deal with vulnerability and tenderness.

Not only are men and women biologically different, our attitudes to sex also vary significantly. To men it is more physical, to women more emotional. Men would rather do it than talk about it; women want it to be meaningful most of

SEXUALITY

the time. However, I think women are just as capable as men of having sex without love and enjoying promiscuity. Those of the fairer sex who insist this isn't so have just been conditioned to believe that women shouldn't feel that way. It's an age-old debate as to whether sex and love are the same thing. Each has its own characteristics and can be experienced separately but, when combined, give us our best possible connection with another. Even in a loving relationship we sometimes feel more sexual while at other times more loving and then occasionally, if we're lucky and open to it, the two meet and we have our special encounters of intimacy.

On the whole, men are more at ease with their sexuality because they're allowed to be. Women are more self-conscious about being sexual creatures and either cover it up or wear their sexual allure like a badge of honour. None of this is necessary. True sexuality shines out from within when it is free and unfettered.

As a man you can be many things, including sexual. Enjoy it as a free gift of nature. It is not a complicated thing in itself — we human beings complicate it. Talking about it all the time and boasting about your conquests is a sure sign that you're not at peace with your sexualness. Just accept it and get on with it as well as all the other enjoyable things in your life. In that way, sex will be relaxed for you and not the stress pitfall it often turns out to be.

Worrying about such things as penis size, performance, the woman's pleasure, positions, how long it's lasting and so on actually detracts from the sharing of what should be an entirely enjoyable experience, whether orgasm is reached or any new positions tried. Switch off your brain and your fears, trust yourself and your feelings and begin to enjoy a level of sex you have only dreamed of before now.

Positive self-talk

- I own and enjoy my sexuality.
- I am open to the idea of sex as a creative and spiritual, as well as a physical, experience.
- I own and enjoy my sensual and sexual fantasies, without trying to live them out.
- I accept responsibility for my darkest desires and free my life.
- I do not criticise or doubt myself.

Chapter 9

WORK AND WELL-BEING

I've chosen to talk about work and well-being together because these two aspects of life are interlinked and have a direct relationship to each other.

WELL-BEING

It must be obvious to anyone that stress is a natural consequence of poor health and vice versa. Throughout the book, I have explained that the effects of stress are often covert and make inroads into various other areas without warning. So apparently, overnight, you can find yourself with a serious health problem you weren't aware you had. That's why I emphasise prevention and maintaining a stress-managed life style. It's impossible to separate ourselves into compartments — the stress you create in one area is bound to affect others and your overall well-being.

I prefer 'well-being' as a concept to health or fitness because it is a more comprehensive word, taking in emotional, spiritual and psychological aspects of life as well as physical. Also, health means the absence of illness, and fitness means strength and prowess, neither of which means anything in stress terms. Lots of men who think they're healthy and fit are labouring under a huge stress burden. The incidence of the fifty-year-old executive, who jogs every morning and thinks of himself as 'fit', dropping dead suddenly of a heart attack is so common it has become a cliche in our society. Everything I write about in this book is essentially about well-being. There are, however, some specific issues that have not as yet been covered.

Food-traps

There's nothing I can tell you about diet that you won't have heard from a hundred nutritionists but in terms of stress there are certain factors to keep in mind when eating. Addiction to various foods is very common and, by examining what these foods contain, you can work out quite easily what your personal food-traps are. High-sodium, high-fat, low-fibre meals are best kept to a minimum but it's good for the soul, if not the body, to indulge in them occasionally. I'm a great believer in cutting down rather than cutting out. Depriving yourself of foods you really enjoy can actually cause stress.

As with all stress management, balance is the key. Watch your food and drink each day and 'listen' to your body. If you suddenly get a craving for an apple, there's probably a good nutritional reason for it. That's not to say you should have one on the hour every hour just because you feel like it. That's the point. Everything in moderation is okay even so-called 'bad food'.

Keep in mind that a lot of our eating is habitual, for example, we don't always eat because we're hungry. Eating in our society is also done for emotional reasons, pleasure, socialising and in association with certain behaviours. I know that the minute I hit the beach, I feel like eating a pie because we always used to eat pies at the beach when I was a child. Fairs mean fairy floss, shopping must include a cappuccino and what would a movie be without popcorn? We have simply built up these needs from years of conditioning and there's nothing wrong with it as long as we are aware. Eating mindlessly is a dangerous habit as, eventually, you stop monitoring what you eat altogether, you get lazy about it and over time this can make you very sick.

Certain foods can cause stress, for instance high-sugar items can get you over-excited and agitated so that rest and relaxation are more difficult. When you eat, therefore, also becomes a crucial factor. Taking coffee, sweet drinks and other sugar products late at night is inadvisable for this reason and it may even interrupt your sleep. Addiction to coffee, tea, chocolates and cakes, just to name a few common items, is very tough on the nervous system and can exacerbate conditions such as asthma and anxiety; eating too much red meat has been linked to arthritis; too many dairy products clog up the heart.

These are just a few examples and you're better off to let your own common sense guide you. I believe we all know what our individual weaknesses are; it's just a matter of whether we choose to let them be in control or whether we care enough about ourselves to exercise some discipline over our dietary habits. Many food problems amount to a form of slow suicide as is the case with alcohol addiction and cigarette smoking.

Food is basically fuel for the functioning of the body. Most of you would take more care with what you put into your car engine than into your own bodies. We are not automatically entitled to 'three score years and ten' — we have to look after our vehicle and not take it for granted. Many foods actually enhance well-being and promote stress management. Know why you eat the things you do and when, break habits that are harmful and aim for more variety in your food intake. I have to say again that you can break behaviour patterns only when you know where they come from.

Here is a check-list about your diet:

- Why do you have to eat an entire block of chocolate instead of just a few squares? Are you looking for a sugar rush? Is the chocolate compensating for something else you feel lacking in your life?

- When you pass that fast food outlet and just have to go in for that burger or chicken dinner, are you needing a meal or merely responding to an effective advertising campaign?

- When you smother your meal in salt, pepper and sauces without even tasting it, is it because you know the food is bland and tasteless or is it just a habit to go heavy on the seasoning?

- When you eat far more than you need at one sitting or throughout the day, are you really that hungry, are you greedy or were you taught to overeat in your family of origin?

- When you come home from work tired, stressed or depressed, do you reach for convenience comfort foods to cover up your boredom and frustration with life?

These are some sample questions only. You could write dozens of your own but I'm sure you get my message.

Alcohol, drugs and cigarettes

I've listed these addictions together as they've been mentioned before and they're all similar in their addictive properties and creation of stress.

Alcohol is extremely habit-forming and relates directly to emotional problems, chemical addiction and health deterioration. It plays havoc with the nervous system which has to keep adjusting to extreme highs and lows; inebriation and then the coming-down; excitation and then depression — a constant roller-coaster ride. As well as that, alcoholics are often in conflict with themselves and the people around them so stress is an ever-present reality.

Alcohol has its rightful place in our society for pleasure, socialising and cultural interest. Unfortunately, it is a powerful narcotic and takes hold of the addictive personality without warning. You can be hooked right from when you first start drinking as a young man. It's even seen as part of our cultural initiation that a male should go out and get drunk every weekend and booze it up at every given opportunity. This can be the start of a lifetime habit if it is not curbed and kept within reasonable limits. Excess is part and parcel of the teenage experience but it should be seen as a temporary state. If you're in your twenties and beyond, and you still feel the need to go out on a regular basis and get drunk, you could be a borderline alcoholic. There are other give-away signs such as the need to drink every day, sneaking alcohol when you shouldn't be having it, personality changes when you drink and, of course, the volume of alcohol you consume.

Experts believe that alcoholism is a genetic condition and therefore a disease like any other, but I also believe any of us can go from a glass of wine or occasional beer to excessive drinking if we're not careful. Read back over the section in Chapter 3 where I speak of personality types. If you fit the addictive profile, you'll need to be more vigilant with your food and drink intake.

At whatever level your alcohol is affecting you, it is harming you — don't kid yourself that it's okay because you get drunk only once a week or you only drink beer. It doesn't matter. Alcohol is killing you, whether it takes a year or a lifetime. If you can't cut down yourself, get into a programme, find healthier alternatives but most of all, work on the self-sabotage that is at the root of all addictive behaviour.

Drugs come in many forms in our society and it's not only the crazed, high junkie who has a problem. While that's at one end of the spectrum, the average guy can be hooked on pain-killers, tranquillisers, any number of prescription drugs, as well as so-called 'designer' drugs, without anyone knowing about it. In other words, drugs are an insidious problem and often disguised under respectable facades — the housewife on Valium, the uni student on speed, the business executive experimenting with cocaine, the yuppie couple with their grass.

Of course, if the habit gets out of hand, people find out, jobs are lost, sporting glory is stripped away and marriages crack. To me, these are secondary effects. I'm more concerned with the immediate damage to the drug-user. Depending on the choice of drug, the physical and emotional toll is often very great and the resultant stress very high. Limit your intake of all drugs, even the legal ones. Don't get your body used to a narcotic solution being offered every time there is some slight discomfort or pain because, again, this is very habit-forming. There are any number of herbal remedies for everyday problems such as headache, insomnia, body pain and yes, even stress. Most of us are just too lazy to find out; it's easier to reach into the bathroom cabinet for the quick fix which of course is what our society is all about. As life gets more hectic and complex, our society is becoming less and less tolerant of distractions such as the need to sleep, rest, eat properly, exercise and take care of our health. We want everything quickly — immediate and preferably disposable so we don't even have to clean up after ourselves. Who's got time to meditate a headache away when a pain-killer will do the trick in a couple of minutes?

Pain is a message from the body and when you ignore it or cover it up, you are in effect disguising a problem. I'm not suggesting that you should panic every time you get the slightest twinge. In fact, hypochondria and any other kind of focusing on one's health is very stressful and negative. It can even bring on health problems by way of anxiety or self-fulfilling prophecy.

In Chapter 1, I speak about stress in general and the connection between the health of body and mind. It is the chronic condition, the recurring problem, that should alert you. A headache every day isn't normal nor is daily pain or excessive fatigue unless there's a sound medical reason for it. If there isn't, look beyond to the possibility of an emotional cause or stress overload. Correct that rather than fall for the quick-fix solution. Any drug therapy should be short term unless there is a chronic mental or physical disease involved.

So for you and me, other non-medicinal remedies can be found. Pain can be reduced by mind power, deep breathing, meditation, changing the diet, laughter, exercise, relaxation, massage, Reiki, a short holiday and so on and so on. Don't give me the 'too busy' excuse. I just don't accept that as a valid reason for not looking after yourself. If you are intent on living a short, stress-filled, unhealthy life then go on as you are; if you want to live a long life riddled with addiction, pain, emotional unhappiness and stress, then, again, continue as you are, but if you want quality and quantity of life, you need to evaluate your life style habits, including the way you approach food, drink, drugs and addictive substances.

Cigarettes

Now we come to the most addictive drug of all. Cigarette-smoking is accessible, still relatively inexpensive, a badge of sophistication amongst teenagers, if no longer adults. Why is it the most addictive of all commonly available drugs? It is not only the fact that many young people experiment with smoking and, nowadays, other drugs such as grass, speed and ecstasy; it is also because cigarettes hook more than the chemical need they create. It is a multi-faceted addiction as it gets you physically, habitually and emotionally. Cigarettes are deceptively relaxing; in fact, they raise the heart-rate and therefore cause instant stress to the body every time you puff. I don't need to outline the health risks that smoking poses — they're printed on every packet these days.

Just as we drink in relation to a series of social behaviours, smokers tend to light up at specific times — unless they're chain-smokers who never stop! If you're a smoker, think about it — when do you reach for a cigarette habitually? When you are out drinking, after a meal and after sex. There are also many theories around the fact that cigarettes provide an outlet for oral gratification, being put to the mouth as a nipple or thumb is. I don't know how helpful psychological explanations are in this case. What is far more significant is that doctors tell us it's the hardest addiction to give up.

Ideas for quitting abound. Some suggest slow withdrawal with the help of nicotine patches, special chewing gum, 'Quit' programmes, substitutes like sweets or exercise and lots of will-power. Other experts say nothing works as effectively as stopping cold-turkey. There'll be withdrawal pangs and behavioural change no matter how you choose to quit so I guess it's a matter of choosing your own preferred method. If you can get away from your usual environment and out of your usual routine it's easier; faced with the same everyday stresses and strains it's too easy to just reach for a cigarette again. I would opt for cutting down to give the body a chance to adjust and then joining a support group if you can so you don't have to go it alone. An incentive such as a health reason or desire for sporting fitness helps as does a supportive partner.

Whatever is the most painless way is the best. In giving up cigarettes, you are losing a friend, a support, so take it easy and be patient with yourself. It is such a difficult thing to do that you have to be really motivated. Some quitters opt for hynotherapy to reach the subconscious desire to smoke and remove it. Another therapy that is recording high levels of success is kinesiology. This treatment utilises the body itself to access the reason for the addiction and then removes physically and emotionally the dependence on cigarettes.

Exercise

I cited exercise as a key stress management tool in Chapter 1 as it not only raises general fitness, it reduces physical tension and relieves accumulated stress in the body. If it's enjoyable, you're getting the benefits of a pleasurable activity as well and, in my opinion, one of the best ways to cut down stress is to enjoy yourself. Even work and chores can be fun with the right attitude as we shall see in the next section and the next chapter.

I don't have much more to add in regard to exercise except that it should be regular, suited to your life style and pleasant. I'm afraid I don't go for the 'no pain, no gain' theory. Unless you're in training for a sporting competition, or you're a body-builder, exercise should not have to be tough or expensive. Fancy gym memberships and special clothing will not help you to get fit. Keep it simple: a brisk walk and a few laps of swimming every week.

Exercise should be part of an overall regime of getting and keeping fit. The problem is you guys can get obsessive about it and the next thing you know your exercise programme is causing you stress! Jogging for instance can become incredibly addictive so all you've done is swap one addiction for another if you give up smoking and then jog seven mornings a week. Moderation, moderation, moderation — no matter how boring that sounds. Have passion in what you do by all means but channel it evenly around the various areas of your life so that you're not doing one or two things excessively and neglecting twenty other things that are also important.

Sleep

Sleep is a great healer and a daily gift of revitalisation. Again, it is a perfectly natural thing so why do a lot of guys have difficulty with it?

The most common cause of insomnia, apart from physical reasons such as eating too much at bedtime, drinking coffee before sleep or chronic pain/discomfort, is anxiety. The first thing you need to identify, if you are suffering insomnia on a regular basis, is what's causing it. If there is no obvious reason, then let me suggest the following — overly active mind, high stress, anxiety, a situation in your life that you can't get a handle on.

There are two specific types of insomnia: where you can't get to sleep, or where you drop off easily but then keep waking during the night. Interrupted sleep is actually far less restful than a few quality hours. If it's the first variety, I would hazard a guess that you are not relaxed enough when you hit the sheets. A relaxation tape, some warm milk, soothing music or a few light exercises will help but the most important rule is to leave your day's concerns and stresses outside the bedroom door. Worrying about things or planning strategies for the next day will serve only to waken you up or ensure that any sleep you do get is fitful and unsatisfying.

With a decent night's sleep, you can wake to your challenges or difficulties refreshed and ready to begin again. That's probably why we need sleep: it is not only a biological necessity but a psychological one. Imagine having to live day by day, relentlessly on, without a break. Sleep deprivation is a well-known torture and research shows that after a sufficient length of time without sleep, human beings display psychotic behaviour. On a smaller scale, we all know how irritable we are after even one night's poor sleep and how our powers of concentration suffer.

The type of insomnia that keeps waking you up all night, or occurs when you've only slept a few hours and then suddenly you find yourself wide awake at three in the morning, is brought on by not sleeping deeply enough. You were so tired you dropped straight off but you weren't really getting quality sleep so a little sound or disturbance woke you and then your mind took over with all its hidden fears and dark thoughts.

The trick is to prepare yourself properly for sleep in the first place. Never just drop into bed after a tough day without unwinding. It's essential to create a hiatus between work and bed. Leisure is a necessity, not a luxury. If you read or watch TV, try not to think about anything stressful as it's just as important to relax the mind as the body. Try to cut off from work or worries for a period of time before preparing for bed and get under the covers in the most relaxed mood possible. If you're with someone else, you may have to compromise on such matters as when the lights go off or whether you make love but that's fine as long as you don't get into hassles — the worse thing you can do prior to sleep.

Get into a sleeping ritual so that your mind knows when you're ready to sleep: turn off the light, relax your body, clear your mind and peacefully expect to sleep. Never, never get anxious about the time or how many hours it is before you have to get up, a sure recipe for insomnia.

Dreams

Dreams are a particular fascination of mine and I talk about the subject every chance I get. If you are particularly interested in it there are many good books around but join a dream group if you can because working with your dreams day after day will bring you many benefits.

Many people find their dreams so confusing that they either fail to remember them or they cannot understand them. That's because dreams come to us in symbolic language and are direct messages from the subconscious.

They help us in a number of ways — releasing fears, anxieties, pressures, feelings that may be hidden or unknown to us in waking life, healing deep-seated psychological problems by bringing them into our awareness, helping us to access insights and messages from the subconscious mind. Precognitive dreams can offer omens for the future including warnings, premonitions, and predictions, allowing us to conjure up fantasy images such as dream lovers, travel, wealth, power, and so on. We can test out our feelings through dream experiences and work out problems with loved ones or absent friends.

Dream research is staggering these days. It indicates that the line between conscious and subconscious is very thin indeed. You get to decide what you want to dream about and how dreaming can benefit you. This is called dream 'incubation' and is very easy to do with practice. For example, if you want an answer to a nagging problem, you only have to ask your subconscious to work on it during the night and you'll have a solution in the morning. Unfortunately, it won't necessarily come in a very clear form and it might take a bit of effort to decipher its meaning. That's why the more you work with your dreams on a daily basis, the better.

There are two categories of dreamers — recallers and non-recallers. If you fall into the first category, you are probably a seeker of truth, you want to know what makes you tick, you like to discuss issues and think deeply. If you are a non-recaller, you may scoff at metaphysical or spiritual pursuits, preferring to concentrate on material reality. Non-recallers even have a faster eye-blink rate during sleep, as if trying to shut out the dream images!

Your dreams are still benefiting you whether you remember them or not but, obviously, you can get a lot more direct help if you know what your key issues are. Recurring dreams are a particular fount of information because the persistent messages and images are pointers to things you need to look at in your waking life. Nightmares are the same except that they relate directly to fears you need to release. Deal with the source of the fear when you're awake and you will stop having the same scary dreams.

If you decide you'd like to work with your dreams, buy a simple note-pad that you can use as your dream journal. Keep it by your bedside and write down everything you can remember as soon as you wake up. At first, there'll only be sketchy recall but as your subconscious mind begins to realise you're serious, you'll get clearer and clearer images. Interpreting the meanings also becomes easier. Then you can start to experiment, have some fun, create a dream lover, solve your decision-making dilemmas, and explore your inner realms via the rich source of material that makes up your dream world.

MENOPAUSE

Before I leave the subject of well-being I want to pursue the controversial question of whether there is such a thing as male menopause. I think there is and that it differs from female change of life only in that it's not biological, at least not in such an obvious sense. It is emotional but it rightly belongs in this chapter because it has to do with male development stages and that involves health.

Menopause marks an ending and a beginning. For women, it occurs anywhere from the late thirties to the fifties. Men seem to go through their 'mid-life crisis' after they turn forty. It probably has something to do with farewelling youth, grasping at one last bite of the cherry, redefining personality, goals, achievements and so on. Often it means a spiritual journey but sometimes it involves tremendous physical and practical change. So many men run off with younger women at this time in their lives that it's become a standing joke in our society. It's good to take stock of our lives as we go along and at particular crossroads. It doesn't necessarily require radical upheaval.

This is a particularly vulnerable time for your health if you are a man as your life style to date could be rearing up to haunt you — all those good intentions you didn't keep to, the rest you didn't take, the improved diet you didn't maintain, the stress you didn't reduce.

No matter what your age as you read this, you can make positive changes. Follow the suggestions given chapter by chapter in this book, examine the negative aspects of your current life and make a start. It all begins with one small step in the right direction. Don't let the statistics frighten you: you are not a statistic, you are an individual with power and choices. You can get well if you want to, give up smoking, drink less, eat better, have more joyful relationships, enjoy your work whatever it is and live a longer, happier life. Believe it — that's what it takes. I always say that to improve your life you need desire and a plan of action. Well I'm supplying the plan but you need the desire to start with, and then act! Soon, your life will reflect back to you your new and improved thinking, feeling and behaviour. This book is a blueprint and it'll be as successful as you intend it to be.

Stress management is about health — total health, and that translates into well-being.

AGEING

Ageing creates a lot of stress for men as indeed it does for women. Our society worships the young and beautiful so our fear is that in getting older, we might lose our appeal sexually and in other ways. I can't say the idea of wrinkles, joint pains and grey hair exactly grabs me but I think of life as a series of stages. The mature years are simply another level of experience and even death, when the time is right, will be natural and appropriate. What is there to fear? The fear of death is the same as all the other fears discussed in this book — fantasy. We fear what we imagine because we have no tangible proof of what it is. That does not mean it's necessarily going to be horrible. It may be a glorious experience — who has ever come back to say? Those who purport to have had a near-death experience or 'clinical' death say the predominating feature is peace and calm. Maybe we finally just meet our inner selves, which is what we can do in life if we try. It's just another attitude. Death is regarded as loss and an ending rather than a whole new beginning. Even if you don't believe in the continuity of the spirit, you can still accept that your death will merely be the conclusion of your live and to be neither rejoiced over nor dreaded, just accepted as an inevitable fact.

Plan for a peaceful ending to your life and that's what you'll have. Live your life well and you can't have anything else. You do not have to die of a cruel disease or have a sudden heart attack or lose your life in a horrible accident, no matter what the statistics tell you.

Ageing is the most natural process of all. You've all heard it said that you start dying from the moment of your birth and of course that is true. Why not turn that around and see it as *living* from the moment of your birth? We're not automatically entitled to 'three score years and ten' — some of us live to be 100 and others die as children. There are no rules about this and you only feel deprived if you try to force your own timetable and plans onto universal laws. Live every moment — that's all you do own. Then it will no longer matter if you are thirty or fifty or eighty. You'll enjoy what that period of your life has to offer. If you think of yourself only as your physical body then as it ages, and is no longer as beautiful or efficient, you will feel less of a person. Focus only on your inner beauty which never ages and never dies.

One particular factor of ageing that affects you guys in particular is baldness. Even young men can lose their hair, I realise, but this condition is often regarded as a loss of youthfulness and a sign of premature ageing. There are many aids and treatments on the market to help you with the physical aspects of baldness but psychologically, you have to decide if you will let hair or the absence of it affect your self-esteem and confidence. A woman who would let your thinning hairline stop her going out with you is not much of a catch, is she? Of course, if you feel less about yourself, you can only attract women who will also reject you as you are rejecting yourself. Make the best of your appearance whether you have hair or not, or you could go the other way and have the rest shaved off. Bald men are seen as pretty sexy these days! Just remember not to invest in superficial factors about yourself and ageing will not be a stressful problem; instead it will just be part of the overall journey.

WORK

What do you think of when you think of 'work'? A chore? A necessary evil? Something unpleasant?

I'm going to ask you to put aside any preconceived ideas you might have about work before you dive into this chapter. There's no doubt that you would have set ideas about this subject. It's not a topic that people feel neutral about. They're either wrapped up in their jobs or they hate them. It's a bit like taxes — inevitable and a great source for whingeing.

The work ethic is alive and well in Australia, despite our popular images of sunny beaches, high unemployment rates and a national laid-back attitude. It may not be as entrenched as in previous generations because young people today want life style as much as careers and employment opportunities are harder to find; also, we live in a time of instant gratification. Even motivated youngsters find it hard to battle through several years of studying, apprenticeships and waiting on jobs when the immediate pleasures of life beckon.

Whether you are working full time or have chosen an alternative path, what I'm going to say about work affects you as I'm speaking much more broadly than just about paid employment or working to earn money. I'm more interested in work as a social concept and as a philosophy because we've all been hoodwinked for decades into believing that life 'wasn't meant to be easy' and that's supposed to include work. Why can't work be easy and fun and joyful? The famous poet and philosopher, Kahlil Gibran, says that if you hate your work it's better for you to sit at the temple gates and beg for your daily bread and let those who work with love get on with it. Translated into modern terms that means going on the dole, which is becoming a permanent solution for a whole section of the community that is chronically unemployed.

Unemployment

The unemployed are perceived as a sub-culture in our society, one that is viewed with a high degree of contempt because, as with so many labelled groups I've cited in this book, they get lumped into one stereotyped category.

If you are currently unemployed, whether temporarily or long term, do not allow yourself to be pigeon-holed in this way. Poor self-image is one of the greatest handicaps to successful job-seeking so don't fall into the trap of feeling less valuable because you're on the dole or you can't find work. In a society that worships status and wealth, a person who doesn't work is regarded as a threat to things conventional, a 'waster' and valueless. Get out from behind these labels for only you can agree to wear them or choose to discard them. Feel good about yourself, speak positively about your situation, for instance if anyone asks say you're 'job-seeking' rather than unemployed.

The question that's usually asked of a stranger after his name is 'what do you do fo a living?' If you don't have a satisfactory answer, you are dismissed and that can be soul-destroying to one already fighting off the ravages of low self-esteem. Expect this attitude and be prepared to be proud of yourself without defensiveness or aggression. You are valuable no matter what you do. If you sincerely don't want to be part of the rat-race, find a viable alternative by which you can fulfill yourself and give back to your community.

We can no longer operate within a narrow definition of work. Having a nine-to-five job does not mean what it used to. Under the working umbrella is a multitude of choices — full-time, part-time, casual, shared jobs, shifts, just to name a few. Then there are other umbrellas that cover a whole range of alternatives that broaden the concept of 'work'. For example, there is a fast-growing body of workers that don't get paid yet give tirelessly to their communities — volunteers. There are also people who work for payment other than cash, exchanging goods and services on a shared arrangement. And let us not forget the millions of housewives and house-husbands in this country who work 24-hour shifts and either get no payment or manage on a small pension or allowance. Also, there are artists of every kind and sportspeople who live on grants or work part-time to support their talents and ambitions.

Ultimately the onus is on the individual to make something of his own life so, if you are out of work at present, look carefully at your options and whatever you do don't become negative, a seductive trap and so much easier than fighting for change and improvement.

Look in the papers and job centres for openings but also write letters of application to places where you'd like to work, use lateral thinking in regard to opportunities, be creative, do volunteer work which can often turn into paid employment, find odd jobs in your local neighbourhood for some extra money, be too busy for self-pity and negative thinking. Take as many free courses as you can manage in order to improve your attractiveness as a job candidate, don't get discouraged even if you have to attend a hundred unsuccessful job interviews, believe there is the right job waiting for you somewhere out there and keep putting out for it. Remember desire, plan, action. Do one positive thing every day towards getting work if that's what you want and never give up. There are dozens of organisations and schemes available these days to help the unemployed of all ages — use them and never see yourself as a failure.

Employment

Whether you've been working for a year or thirty years, your attitude to your job will be the determining factor in how satisfied you are, creatively, emotionally and financially. The work ethic promotes the idea that all work is noble and must be done, no matter how awful or demeaning. As an ex-workaholic I used to buy that wholly but I no longer support the work ethic. There is no intrinsic value in working for its own sake.

You are just as valuable when you are sitting on a beach watching a sunset or weeding a garden or working at a desk. We live in a capitalist society that teaches the lesson: productivity is everything. At the end of every day I used to ask myself what I had achieved that day. Now I ask myself what I have learnt and what joy I have experienced. It's a whole different perspective. I work less hard but still achieve a prodigious amount of work some days, and nothing at all on other days — it all balances out but the key difference is I'm no longer a stressaholic, I'm no longer chronically ill and I enjoy all the work I do.

If I were to tell you that you could learn to live your life in such a way that you would no longer differentiate between work and play, you'd probably scoff and call me an impractical fool. Well, you can and still make good money and get heaps done. It's all about the old saying, 'work smart not hard.' The answer is to stop categorising your life. Let the boundaries fall. Be just as happy in the office as you are on the golf-course or working around the house. Become a total person. Job labels are amongst the most insidious as so many people use their jobs to identify themselves, especially you guys. You are not plumbers, doctors, accountants or technicians — they are your jobs. If you see yourselves and these occupations as the one and same thing, you disappear and become something that is permanently outside yourself, an external reality that is separated from your true essence.

Becoming one with one's work is a real danger and explains the high incidence of men dropping dead soon after retiring. When the job is over, these men lose their sense of identity and worth, thus the meaning of life. Retirement should be planned for and filled with joyful new things, adventures and beginnings. It should never be seen as an ending or a form of death: symbolic death can easily translate into the real thing. Never underestimate the power of the mind (as we shall see in the next chapter).

Workaholism

As with other forms of addiction, the same issues apply — work becomes a source of self-value and is then taken to extremes to compensate for feelings of inadequacy and other emotional problems. Like addiction to stress, this is a very subtle form and takes over before you realise how serious it's become. It has nothing to do with diligence or putting in extra hours. It is obsessive preoccupation with work, inability to take rest periods, feeling that nothing is as important.

As stated in the initial discussion on stress, balance is vital so that energy is spread out over the whole day's commitment and sufficient time is allotted for leisure and rest. Some men can't even play sport without being obsessive about it and this behaviour carries into retirement so that, instead of being a gentle period of sharing with family, travel, hobbies, etc., it's just another form of stress!

One of the complaints I hear most from wives is that their husbands are too caught up in work and spend too much time out of the home. When I ask the husbands about it they see it as necessary to keep up in this competitive world and care for their families adequately. That's fine but your families want you alive and well, not absent and heading for an early grave.

Apart from cutting down your workload, which may not be possible, there are other ways to be kinder to yourself:

- Firstly, look at your reasons for working so hard. In my case, I had been brought up by an over-achieving mother who taught me by example and words that work, success and accomplishment are everything. Luckily my body kept breaking down until I listened and changed my life before I developed cancer or some other serious disease. The word 'disease' comes from two words, dis-ease, when the body is out of harmony with itself and continually breaks down. If we don't heed the small warnings, we eventually have to get very sick and stop altogether. In this way illness can be a blessing but I would prefer to see you take preventative measures. I said at the start of the chapter that work and stress are linked. Your attitude to work will make the difference between whether you run yourself into the ground for forty years working for basic money or enjoy a nice lifestyle along the way and retire happy.

• Secondly, look at all your needs on a daily basis as I suggested earlier in the book. Don't just persist with the attitude that you'll catch up. You can't catch up time, joy, love, family. Take time out to just be. It's frightening to see how many of my clients seem to put their lives on hold year after year, always believing they'll get back to it. If you're like that, look back occasionally to make sure your wife, kids, home and friends are still there. It's easy to lose them and yourself in the shuffle. When all's said and done, what are you going to most remember on your death-bed — how much money you earned every year or who you shared your life with?

The irony is that you can have it all, with a few shifts of attitude and practical changes.

• Thirdly, manage your time so that everything that matters gets a look in. Prioritise from day to day. You can't give equal time to all your commitments each day — that would be impossible but learn to judge what to leave in and what to leave out. The biggest clue to workaholism is when work claims the lion's share of your time and attention. For short bursts such as stocktake time or sales or end of financial year, fine, but watch for those insidious patterns that wind their way around your life until you are their slave.

• Lastly, always break up your day so that there is a hiatus between work and leisure, no matter how short a time.

e cardinal rules are: do not bring work home on a gular basis, do not let work intrude on your private life; turn off that mobile phone occasionally; do totally meaningless things every so often to remind yourself that life is for enjoyment. Yes, workaholics, in case this is the first time anyone's put that to you since you were a kid, life is for fun.

Now, we're going to find out how to make all of your life fun, not just the fun bits!

Attitude to work

To begin, are you in the right job? Many of you probably fell into the jobs you're in when you left school and you've been there ever since. Those of you who are new to the workplace may have chosen a particular career path for the wrong reasons such as money, status, parental approval, easy course of study, friends in same industry, entering family business, and so on. These are the right reasons if the job is right for you but if you've been pressured into it or have drifted into it or it's not your first choice, you're settling for less and you'll never be happy. Here's a good saying: 'If you want to be happy for a year, win Lotto; if you want to be happy for life, find a job you love.'

It doesn't matter what the job itself is as long as you enjoy it — after all, you're going to spend a lot of your days there. Another saying is, 'Do what you love and the money will follow.' Most of you are starting at the wrong end, looking at the end result instead of where everything begins — with yourself. Really look at what you're good at, what you enjoy and build your occupation around that. Not practical? How many dreamers have made their millions because they had the guts to follow their dreams and not spend their lives in a dead-end job, believing their dreams aren't practical?

Who says the practical is better than the dream anyway? Our forefathers, who could not possibly visualise the world of today with its infinite possiblities.

Obviously we can't all be musicians, famous scientists or brain surgeons but be the best at whatever your job is and do it with love. The way I hear people growling about going to work day after day, it's a miracle they don't drop dead sooner from stomach ulcers, cancer, heart attacks and other toxic ailments. Whatever you have to do — cleaning out public toilets, moving furniture, pulling out teeth, washing animals, cooking meals — find a way to do it with joy. Some suggestions are: music, laughter, conversation, humour, pride of accomplishment, sharing, taking pleasure in the work itself. A friend of mine was hauled into the matron's office at the hospital where she works and told off for being too happy! I was myself repeatedly on the carpet as a high school teacher for having too much laughter coming out of my classes.

To motivate people in any field, you need a bright personality and a cheerful disposition. You sell a lot more with a smile than a frown; if you're a teacher, your students are much more inclined to listen if you capture their interest first; even solitary jobs like plumbing or technical work can be improved with a cheery attitude. As you will see in the next chapter, I am not talking about putting on a false act. That would not make any real impact on your overall belief system about work. The changes need to run far deeper.

Work is just another core belief you learnt from childhood and most likely garnered from your parents' values in this area. If you saw your father go out to work every day with a long face and come home with an even longer one, what do you think you might've learnt about work? Release this pattern as you have to with the ones on relationships, love, attitude to self, money, home, family, etc.

Start again with your own relevant choices and behaviours in the present moment.

Whenever I suggest to a client that he's in the wrong job, I get the 'I can't leave work, I have a family to support' speech. There are ways to make changes without jeopardising your life style. But first, you have to know what you want. If you've always wanted to write a novel, for instance, do it in your spare time and try to sell it to a publisher, or attend a writing class, talk to published authors, listen and learn and follow your destiny.

If your dream is not so clear-cut, you just know you hate your current job or you see no chance of advancement, learn a new skill or trade, go and get vocational testing, consult organisations and consultants that advise people on career change. Don't wait till you're sixty and all used up to say you wish you had done something about it sooner.

You have a right to enjoy work — 'enjoy' is not a dirty word. If all else fails, find something you love to do or make or share and turn it into a money-making proposition. Remember 'Trivial pursuit' began as a fun idea in the minds of three friends who devised the game in a lounge room over a few drinks. I don't need to tell you about the success of that venture.

Whatever you want to try, don't let your own self-doubt or the negative thinking of others stop you. There is no failure in trying even if you don't get the desired result at first.

Success

The first thing you have to ask yourself here is by whose standards do you want to be judged — yours or society's?

By society's standards, you are a success only if you have a high-paying status job or at least a regular one, money in the bank, a steady relationship and own lots of material assets. These are all good but hollow victories if you are not a success in your own eyes. If you see yourself as a success, you could be homeless, penniless, loveless and friendless — it wouldn't matter in terms of your own sense of self-value. If you are going to be a derelict in the park, be a good one, the best one you can be and do it with flair and joy. I'm being facetious but it's not far off the truth.

If you are in self-love, however, your life has to reflect it and you will have worldly success as a natural consequence of being who you are — if you want it. If you don't, you won't. You decide.

Many so-called successful people are in fact not truly so because they're not happy. How can anyone profess to be successful who is not happy? It's illogical in my mind.

What is happiness, you ask, and is it really attainable? Most definitely and much of Chapter 10 is devoted to this subject. In terms of work, I think a happy garbologist is far more successful than a miserable solicitor. Success means a sense of satisfaction that you have done your best every day, that you have been honest in all your dealings, that you enjoy the way you earn your daily bread, that you have not deliberately hurt anyone and you are at peace with yourself.

Money

Money is nice. It buys lots of things we want, it offers a desirable life style and it gives us freedom and choices. It is not the root of all evil nor does it have the power to make or mar happiness. These are qualities with which we've endowed money — in itself it has no intrinsic value other than its buying power.

So why then does money, or the lack of it, control our lives as much as it does? Of course you know I'm going to say it's attitude and social opinion. Our society attributes so many emotions and abilities to money that a shortage of this commodity causes more than just practical hardship — it's become associated with self-esteem, value, image, power and ideas about success/failure. It follows then that a person with money feels empowered, important, successful while a person who has a low earning capacity feels the opposite way about themselves.

Money is one of the most addictive substances around — people kill for it, die for it, make love for it, betray for it, and certainly get sick for it. To keep it in perspective, think of it in the same light as all the other factors we've discussed. It is an external thing and has nothing whatever to do with you as a person. You are neither better nor worse because you have money or don't. Lots of terrific people are poor and lots of awful people are rich. It's how you regard your wealth and what you do with it that counts. If you work hard you have a right to your Mercedes, mansion, holidays abroad and expensive life style. Yet lots of people work hard and never attain these riches for a variety of reasons.

So why envy others? Enjoy what you have, and remember that many things are free and available — good health, the air, the beaches, the sun, sky and stars, true friends, love, fun, conversation, walks, music, laughter — the list is endless. Expensive dinners out, fancy clothes, holidays and other material things are terrific but shouldn't be anyone's life ambition. They certainly shouldn't own you and rule you.

Have you ever asked yourself what drives a man to make his millions or establish a big corporation or become rich and powerful in the business world? How much money can one spend or use in a lifetime? Perhaps a better question to ask is how much security can wealth and position buy? How much you have in assets or cash in the bank will never make you secure. Paul Lowe, an international personal development lecturer, says that in all his travels working with people, even those dying of AIDS and suffering from any number of other illnessses and emotional pain, he never found a group of people more unhappy or insecure than the Hollywood movie star community. It's not hard to see why: their whole lives are external, determined by image, appearance, money, status, success, peer approval. They spend all their days waiting for the phone to ring so that they know they're loved and wanted. The more money they make, the more they spend and still they cannot feed the hunger inside that keeps them feeling constantly empty.

If those of you who are wealthy and successful were willing to get off the treadmill for a few minutes and listen to what I'm saying, maybe you could admit to yourselves that you're not really happy despite your position and money.

Am I saying that it's better to be poor, that there's something essentially noble about struggling for money day after day? NO. I am saying, do not identify with your material possessions. They are simply in your life for your use, to serve a practical purpose. It's so easy to get lost in the cars, houses, equipment, clothing and other trappings of life that should just be there for appreciating and enjoying.

The material in the next chapter will make clearer a lot of what I'm saying here but it's important right now that I share a little of my personal journey and philosophy regarding money. It would be easy for you to think I am expounding theories from a privileged position when in fact, I live these beliefs every day. I was brought up by a successful working woman who always taught me that there are no limits, that there's no such word as 'fail,' and what you work for and achieve in life is paramount. Through this influence, I grew up to become a stressed-out overachiever. I accomplished a lot but I was a control freak and a perfectionist.

When I was a teacher, I was tied to a pay packet, mortgage, bills, loans, paying off a car — the whole bit, and I saw my security as these things. I thought nothing of working sixteen-hour days, it made me feel important and worthwhile. As long as I was helping others and punishing myself, I felt I was living out my life-purpose. I'll bet many of you feel that way now and live lives of 'quiet desperation' because you don't see an alternative. I couldn't either but I changed my direction in the early 1980s without realising that I was moving away from everything familiar. From a secure job base, I jumped out into the unknown and I'm still out there! But the essential difference is that I'm no longer scared.

In our society, it's very difficult to operate in financial insecurity as we are set up to believe that we must be insured, superannuated and — my favourite — have money put by for 'a rainy day'. I guarantee that if you have money put by for a rainy day, that rainy day will come! Why not save for a sunny day, for holidays and luxuries — why do we always presume that bad days are on their way? A friend taught me a terrific affirmative saying for every morning on waking: 'Something wonderful's going to happen for me today'.

Say that on a daily basis and you watch what happens. Give up saying the famous one — 'shit happens' — the subconscious has no sense of humour. It takes you literally. If it thinks you expect trouble, it'll obediently supply it by the bucketload. (But more of that in the next chapter.)

The point of my story is that I went from someone who knew exactly where she stood financially and always had her bills paid up in time to a person living permanently out on a financial limb. I'm still a good money manager, or I couldn't survive but I've put my dream before security, freedom before safety. For years after I started on this path, I used to joke that my post office box was my bank because whatever came in the mail was my income. It took years to get past the fear of living like this and develop a level of faith that I'm always okay. I see money for what it is now and whatever I have in my wallet, be it five cents or $100, is okay. Gradually, the situation is turning around. The more you trust, the more you have — and it's without the stress, control, illness and worry. I roll with the financial punches. Some weeks, I'm rolling in money and other weeks, I'm skint. I see no difference in these two scenarios other than my buying less on the lean weeks. I have a roof over my head and nice things that I paid for years ago, I've never missed a meal and I go out when I can. I've set my priorities and made my choices, and so can you. Having a family that you're responsible for is no excuse to give up on your dreams. Those of you are who are self-employed know exactly what I've been talking about. And if you're unhappily employed, I beg you to look at other options. Continuing in a job that you hate is slow death.

My overall message about money is to balance what you have with what you need — pay the essentials first, then whittle down your other commitments, put some aside and enjoy the rest! You could have a million dollars in the bank and still feel 'poor'. It's what we call 'poverty consciousness'. With this type of limited thinking, you are going to keep driving yourself to earn more and save more because you feel constantly insecure. You are your own security, your only security, and once you know that everything becomes easier.

A final word on money: whatever your income, whether a pension or a billionaire's salary, it's all the same except in your mind. This is where you can be and have anything you can imagine and, as we'll see in the next chapter, that's where it all begins anyway.

The workplace

Stress in the workplace is extremely common because we can't choose our bosses and our co-workers — or can we?

As I tell my clients and students, if you can't change the situation, change your attitude to it. If you have done your 'homework' on yourself you will be in a job you like, working with people you enjoy being around and earning good money anyway. How? You can only attract what you believe you deserve.

Let's retrace our steps to the subject of vibrations. Let's say that you were brought up in a household that believes work is a four-letter word, something to be endured so there's food on the table and the bills are paid. You go out into the world as a job seeker carrying this belief. If your first interview is at a beautiful location, you're offered an office with a view, your co-workers are creative people who want to encourage and support you, your boss is pleasant and undemanding, do you think you'd jump at it as you would a winning lottery ticket? In fact, you'd run a mile, because this job situation does not match your belief system about what a 'job' should be.

Even if you took it, somehow you wouldn't keep it and you'd end up back in a dead-end, poorly paid miserable position which did fit your belief pattern.

So your job reflects a lot about what you think of yourself. Look around you. Are you having hassles with your workmates? Do you feel unappreciated? Is the work repetitive and mind-dulling?

Don't worry. You can change jobs and situations as soon as you're ready to accept happiness! If there's some guy bugging you by the way he works or if a co-worker hogs the credit for your efforts or you have a boss riding you, take the focus away from how awful it all is. Moaning and whingeing promotes negative energy and actually worsen unpleasant situations. If you are in a job environment such as I've described, you are likely to be taking home loads of stress which in turn will have an impact on your personal life and your health. You cannot be responsible for the way others behave, even if it affects you. You can ask assertively for what you need but, once again, the only change you have any power over is in yourself. By changing your thinking, you will view exactly the same situation through new eyes. For instance, if you were to go home from work every day and worry about how the boss doesn't like you, pretty soon you'd expand the anxiety to encompass the possibility of losing your job, then you'd worry about being on the dole, etc, etc. How can you expect to live a stress-free, healthy life like that?

It's crucial to leave work behind, no matter how many hours you work or what the job is. Self-employed people are usually the ones who complain that it's impossible to switch off. You must put yourself before business or customers otherwise you won't be around to take care of either. Set a time for switching off the mobile phone and switching on the answering-machine; if you work with your partner, make a rule not to talk about work at home, especially in the bedroom; allow yourself some down-time every single day, and one day of the weekend should be totally work-free.

You will be more productive, not less, if you follow these suggestions. If there's a workmate you really can't stand, invite him around for a drink or a meal — watch the interaction turn around.

Mateship

Mateship is a huge factor in a man's life even though quite clearly your friendships are very different from the ones women have. As we saw in Chapter 2, the men's movement has altered forever the ways in which males interact. There's always been a level of intimacy but now it's more physical. Touching used to be reserved for the sporting field or you were labelled a 'poofter'. But two men hugging has finally come of age. It's still not on to walk up the street arm in arm as two female friends might but who knows what's round the corner?

Traditionally, men have related on a personal level the way women have. Now you can get together in groups and compare your life-stories and histories but it's still unusual for two mates to meet in a pub for a beer and start yacking about domestic problems as two women would talk over coffee.

Men have fewer friends but tend to keep them longer. (Women, on the other hand, tend to have a whole network of people they can share and interact with.) The bond a man shares with his mate is a very deep one. Workmates sometimes feel like fellow-prisoners, especially in jobs that have an element of sameness, say in a factory or dockyard. Humour becomes an essential ingredient in this type of workplace where individual creativity is not at a premium. On the sporting field men play as one, team members are like brothers and winners are folk-heroes. If a mate's in trouble, a man will bail him out or help unobtrusively — men don't like a fuss at either the giving or receiving end. I feel that sometimes, you men cover up a lot of your deeper feelings by thrashing them out through exercise or laughing them off.

For centuries, women have been angry about oppression and now men together as a brotherhood are vocalising their frustrations and fears in the light of what they no doubt see as their usurped roles. Perhaps the time for resentment is over and now the real work should begin. After revolution comes adjustment to change.

Not only do men have to adapt to a new relationship with women, their man-to-man interactions have altered irretrievably as well. I see nothing negative here. Men now have the potential for a depth of friendship they could not have managed before, either with men or women.

The battle of the sexes still exists and is raging healthily out there but I've always believed that platonic friendship is possible between males and females. Those who say there's always sexuality bristling under the surface are missing the point — friendship and sexuality are not mutually exclusive. The best of lovers are also the best of friends in my view; men and women *can* understand each other. Whatever differences exist are healthy — vive la difference. 'If two people in a relationship are exactly the same, one of them is redundant.' Do you just want to be in love with yourself? There's a lot more to learn when the person you're in love with challenges you and stretches you mentally and emotionally.

So throw away all but the best elements of the concept of 'mateship'. You will find that friendship is all around you in many forms when you're willing to let your guard down and take a chance. Suspicion, self-protective behaviours and cynicism are all stressful elements in life and are no longer necessary when you know you can only attract good into your life.

Winning is a bit like success. It's all very nice to receive peer approval and get praise and acknowledgement but if you're not a winner in your own eyes, you won't get far. There are therapists who specialise in teaching the psychology of winning which mostly involves mind power and confidence (we've examined this in detail in Chapter 1). Power and status symbols are illusions because they exist only in the moment. Self-love lasts a lifetime and no-one can ever take it from you, not even in the darkest place or darkest hour.

Without faith in yourself your successes will be hollow and your victories fleeting. You may even sabotage your own efforts to secure a prosperous life because of your perception that you don't deserve it or your fear of success. Yes, fear of success is very real and prevents many talented people from realising their true potential.

That brings us neatly to the final chapter of the book which summarises everything that's been said and offers you tools for change and growth.

Positive self-talk

- I listen to what my body tells me.
- I honour myself by making time to enhance or restore my well-being.
- I use my dreams to benefit my waking life.
- I act on my desire for a longer, happier life.
- I focus on that part of myself that will not age.
- I never see myself in terms of my paid work or material possessions.
- I do whatever I do with joy.

Chapter 10

POSITIVE LIVING

I want to start off this chapter with a discussion of happiness. This is a very nebulous concept to most people even though we talk a lot about it. Even as we yearn for it, we doubt its existence and certainly we are vague about how to attain it. We know the things that bring happiness but we are not sure what the word itself means. We've all experienced this emotion and we know it feels good but how do we find it and how do we hold onto it once we have it?

More questions than answers? Good. I know then that we have something to learn together. People tell me that men are more practical than women and they will want proof and solutions in this book. I don't necessarily accept that men are more pragmatic than that women are more intuitive but I'll bow to popular convention and say that answers are good as long as we don't insist they're the whole truth. Always keep seeking.

WHAT IS HAPPINESS?

To get the most from this chapter and indeed the whole book, you need to blow away your old ideas about everything that fills your life. A lot of myths surround our understanding of 'happiness'. Here are the main ones:

- Happiness is somehow outside you, and you can get it externally.
- Happiness can be equated with things, people, events, places, conditions, money, etc.
- Things and people can 'make' you happy.
- Happiness is an impossible and that it's not meant to last.
- Happiness is something to aim for as a goal in the future.

Let's explode these myths for a start.

Happiness is inside you and is ever-present, no matter what the external circumstances of your life, so you can never 'get' happy you are already. In this moment of reading, you are as happy as you're ever going to be. Nothing in the future will add one ounce of happiness to your life as you already have an infinite supply. Impossible to believe? It's all there, my friend — you just have to *access* it — a good 1990s word!

If in your mind, happiness is synonomous with a particular thing, say a person, a place, a job, money, a home, travel, sex, a hobby … what happens when you no longer have that thing in your life? Logically, you have to be unhappy. So, you've set yourself up by equating an emotion with an outside object.

Things — or people — can never 'make' you happy. You make yourself happy by reaching within and having a relationship with yourself. Nothing outside you has any power to affect your feelings unless you hand over that power.

Happiness is not only attainable, it is yours forever to keep. It is not a fleeting thing, although most of us experience it that way because that's what we expect. I'm not speaking of riotous pleasure, wild times, hilarious conversations, great company — these can all contribute to happiness but they are only one face of it. True happiness is inner joy and it is continuous. You don't have to do anything, just be, and you have it moment to moment. Any time you want to feel it, you just sit quietly for one moment and you will be able to feel the peace and serenity that resides inside you. Place your hand on the middle of your chest — that's the heart energy centre where you feel love, hurt, fear, vulnerability. When you're feeling anxious or 'unhappy, do this and wait for the energy to change. You can feel it perceptibly, especially with practice.

Deferred happiness is seen as always somewhere off in the future to be looked forward to and worked towards. It's very common in our culture to hear people saying that they'll rest when they have time, they'll travel when they retire; they'll enjoy themselves 'later'. It's continually living in the future, which never actually comes, because once we attain one goal, it's human nature to start aiming for another. So life becomes a series of desires that are just beyond reach instead of a continual manifestation of these.

Okay, let's say I've convinced you. The next obvious question is how you change your thinking about happiness and connect with your inner joy NOW. Apart from all the strategies I've outlined for you in this book already, here are some specfic tools you can use.

Living in the moment

This is tricky for Westerners as we are very goal-oriented and so we're usually running into the future with plans and hopes and desired outcomes. We're also often lost in a past of unfulfilled dreams, old disappointments, frustrations, abandoned hopes and so on. Training ourselves to stay in the present is essential but takes time and patience because we are unlearning the habits of a lifetime. Whenever I feel 'bad', I know I've forgotten to do one or all of the following — to be in the present; to trust; to stay positive.

Living *in* the moment does not mean living *for* the moment. It simply means to enjoy and experience your life intensely in each moment as it passes. Most of us are so busy we're not even aware of being alive, let alone taking in all our experiences fully. The trick is to do one thing at a time, for example I have a habit of watching TV and reading at the same time or washing dishes and listening to music or cooking and talking on the phone, my reason being to save time and prevent boredom. But I have learnt in the course of my own journey over the past three years to focus on what I'm doing and enjoy it even if it's the most mundane task.

By doing this, you can begin to feel very differently about all the things that surround you in your daily life. You'll start to see the magic and the wonder of just being alive instead of looking continually for outside stimulation. Boredom is a fiction of the mind created by the inability to amuse and entertain yourself. Nothing is boring; only people are.

If you can't see what I'm getting at about concentrating on the moment, watch a three-year-old eat an ice-cream. That ice-cream is the whole universe to that child and the pleasure is intense. We have become so jaded because of the sophistication of our society. Get back to simple things and see everything else as a bonus.

Positive thinking

There's been so much said about positive thinking and mind power over the last few decades from Norman Vincent Peale through to the New Age writers of the current time that, again, it's easy to be confused. Does being positive mean that you have to go round grinning all day and see everything as wonderful? Not at all. It is a philosophy, a way of life, a choice. It is often said that we have no power over what happens to us, only our response to it. That's very true. I believe that absolutely everything has a reason and a purpose but we're not aware of it until we look back in hindsight. A friend of mine put it like this: 'In every tragedy there is a gift.' This may seem impossible in the face of some of the awful things that happen to people but there is always a choice of attitude. You create your own reality moment to moment by your thinking or your 'intentions', as Wayne Dyer puts it. Thought creates matter and that's what happens when you manifest a 'self-fulfilling prophecy' — something you predict or expect comes into your physical reality because of the energy you put out. That's why you should be careful what you wish for. You have no control over when things happen and it often appears that we are the victims of bad timing when, in fact, everything happens in perfect time. Your mind is incredibly powerful and you have over 50 000 separate thoughts in a day — if many of these are angry or spiteful or negative, think what you're creating for yourself. Not everyone is prepared to accept total responsibility for the occurrences of their lives — it's much easier to blame God or fate or the government or other people. When you change your thoughts you change your feelings, which in turn changes your behaviour, which then changes your life.

If you believe that life is something that happens to you, you will continue to be a victim, which is in itself an expectation.

Reflections

When we spoke of reflections in the context of relationships, I explained that you receive almost identically what you give out to others. This operates in every area of your life. Think of it this way — imagine you are facing five mirrors, each one representing a key area of your life, the five being home, relationships, money, job, health. What you see in those mirrors is a reflection of who you are, just as you can't look into the bathroom mirror and see Michael Jackson — you can only ever see yourself. So if you don't like what you see in those mirrors — deteriorating relationships, poor health, a job you hate, an uncomfortable home and money problems — it's no use trying to change those external elements. Changing yourself will bring you strong relationships, a better job, improved health, more money and a more suitable house.

Everything begins with your thinking. Most of us only tap into a very small proportion of our mind power. We live in a very negative society and in the main have bought the 'life wasn't meant to be easy' propaganda because we are blocked by fear from believing that life can be easy and smooth and trouble-free. Logically, if you believe that we create everything that happens to us on a daily basis, we can also change it if we don't like it. We are only reluctant to give up control because we sense that at the opposite end of control is chaos, yet I have had more order and harmony in my life since I let go of the reins and let life run its natural course without planning it to the point of destroying all spontaneity, surprise and magic. If you are afraid of words like 'magic', it's because our society teaches that only kooks and religious nuts believe in such a concept.

Immediate reflections of your thoughts are all around you every day — haven't you ever bumped into someone in the street you were just thinking of or wished you could hear from a particular person and they ring you? You can manifest both positive and negative in your life — it's your choice and you are making this choice moment to moment. That's what creating your reality means and the more you become aware of it, the more you will feel your own power.

Choosing a positive life after years of negativity takes determination and practice. Wanting to is enough to get you started. Then build awareness of all the negative thoughts you allow so freely every day. Every time you catch yourself having one of these, gently chide yourself and replace it with a positive thought, for example if you call yourself 'stupid', say no, you're not, and reverse the thought. By this slow but sure method you'll start to make inroads into the layers and layers of conditioned responses that keep you falling back into this habit.

Write down all the areas of life in which you commonly react negatively and next to this list write positive behaviours you could try instead. Be patient with yourself when you have setbacks as you invariably will. Just start again. Every time your life appears to be in the toilet, look for the possible payoff in the current situation as there always is one. Appearances are deceptive and if you refuse to give in to negative thinking or pessimism or doubt or sabotage, you will gain from every experience of your life. I know this all sounds a bit too good to be true. Don't take my word for it — prove it for yourself as I have done. Positive thinking is a practical, workable philosophy that every 'successful' man and woman has employed.

PROSPERITY THINKING

This is a wide umbrella encompassing a range of ideas and skills. You remember we spoke previously of 'poverty consciousness' and 'limitation thinking'? Well, this is the opposite. Prosperity thinking is a pro-active life style and belief system that promotes well-being and success of every kind. It is more than positive thinking which we have already discussed.

Prosperity thinking is not just saying, when bad things happen to me I'm still going to believe that life is good and I'll just start over again. It's going out to create the life you want by utilising specific tools, many of which have already been mentioned in this book. Some other tools are discussed below.

Risk-taking

Risk-taking does not mean foolhardy choices or impulsive behaviour. It means following your intuition even if it goes against your rational judgement. If something feels right, do it. This is also known as 'following your bliss', a Joseph Campbell concept. It means to go in the direction of your love and your joy. As we saw in Chapter 9, a good example is choosing an 'impractical' career such as music or the arts over a 'safe' one. How often we talk ourselves out of what we truly want by a lack of faith in ourselves and in life.

Following your bliss can apply to something as trivial as going to the beach on a hot day instead of mowing the lawn or making a major life decision. I'm not suggesting that you neglect your responsibilities or duties but it's far better to do things out of love than obligation. When you begin to live your life 'prosperously', you will not only do the things you love, you will love the things you do — all of them. Life becomes one long holiday. Instead of waiting for the good things, like going away once a year or getting bonuses, meeting someone special or buying a house, you will live every day as if you already have all these things and more.

But you must learn to back yourself and that requires a good deal of self-trust and courage, especially when you have everyone against you as often happens when you try to do something different. Search your heart for your true desires, make a start and then stick to your guns.

Prosperity does not only relate to money or wealth but every area of your life.

Creative visualisation

This entails imaging in your mind's eye the things you want to bring into your life, working with these images and believing that they are already reality. Let's say you want a red Mercedes.

First, you have to believe you can get one, you deserve one and it's already yours. That's the mind power part of the exercise.

Then you start to cut pictures of these cars out of magazines and stick them everywhere you can — the front of your diary, the fridge door, your bathroom cabinet, use them as bookmarks, whatever. By doing this you are surrounding yourself with the symbology of your desire.

Next, write down every detail of the car you want — the year, the price, the accessories, interior, everything, and pin this list in a very prominent place in your house. Now, every night and morning, close your eyes and imagine that car in its concrete reality. Use each one of your senses — see it, feel what it's like to sit in the driver's seat, smell the upholstery, hear the engine, imagine the feel of driving it, see yourself pulling up in your driveway with it.

Be very specific; for instance, if you visualise the car you want in the showroom, that's where it'll stay. Remember the subconscious is very literal so expect this car in your life.

You don't have to do anything in particular to get the car unless you've got enough money saved up to just go out and buy it. Keep visualising and believing. Ordinary people win cars, inherit money and pick winners every day. Don't concern yourself with the 'how' and the 'when' — that's where most people bog down as such concerns create doubt and get your logical mind back into its old routines.

A friend of mine used this method and got the exact second-hand car he was putting out for, down to the year, colour, make and model, and he paid $200 less than the price he'd visualised!

You can use this tool for almost anything — it just requires trust, determination and sticking to it, no matter how long the object takes to manifest. Many people give up on their dreams because they get tired and discouraged, yet the manifestation may be just around the corner.

Creative visualisation works particularly well for material things but can also bring you a desired lover, job or improved health. It's used extensively in alternative cancer treatment where sufferers visualise the cancer as a 'thing' and then see it reducing in size and finally disappearing. The power of the mind is such that many cancer patients have used this type of meditation successfully. In one documented case, a man in America completely cancelled the malignancy in his body by laughter therapy.

I offer these examples purely for illustrative purposes and I'm not suggesting these extreme cases are applicable to everyone. But some simple uses for creative visualisation are definitely in everyone's reach, for example, visualising a smiling face on a person you're having problems with, seeing yourself hugging someone you don't know how to reach, imagining you have a letter in front of you that offers you a job you covet. By using mind-pictures in this way, your wishes manifest without any physical action on your part other than the original approach such as writing a job application. If the job's right for you and you visualise success, you will see the letter you imagine in your mailbox; you will get a call from the person you've fallen out with and you'll improve your relations with that difficult someone you see smiling in your image.

Try it.

AFFIRMATIONS

This is my personal favourite. I have found saying daily affirmations to be life-changing. There are a few requirements for them to be effective: they must be said in the present tense; they should be said in the first person; and they must be specific. The most important element is emotion — you must feel what you are saying or it has little value.

When you first start saying an affirmation, you are unlikely to believe; that's why it's important to keep working with them over a period of time. It might take months or even years for an affirmation to manifest in a tangible form because you are chipping away at old beliefs and patterns that are deeply ingrained.

Another vital element with affirmations is to work with a few that relate to a particular area of life that you want improved — money, health, relationships, spirituality, work, whatever concerns you most at present. If you just say a jumble of different ones, they'll be meaningless. Here are some suggested ones to get you started.

General: Every day in every way, I'm getting better and
  better and better.

Personal: I love and accept myself in this moment exactly
  as I am,

Money: Money flows freely to me now.

Income: My income increases every day.

Life: Everything comes to me easily and quickly.

Harmony: I am in harmony with everything and everyone around me.

Needs: All my needs are met every day.

Luck: My luck is limitless and comes to me in many different forms.

Health: I am in perfect health.

Prosperity: I embrace my prosperity in all its many forms.

These are very general. The best affirmations are the ones you write for yourself; keep them simple and home in on the issue at hand. If you want to win Lotto, say 'I give thanks for my winnings' — it has to be a 'done deal' in your mind even if you start off just saying the words. If you choose to work with affirmations keep in mind that the 'requests' you make may not come in the form you imagine, for example an affirmation about a win may not be as much as you want or through the obvious source; a statement about work may bring a different job but better than you hoped and ditto for a desired lover.

Like everyone else, I have affirmed for exactly what I've wanted and couldn't get it, but in time I have found the alternative that presented itself was much more right for me. So work with affirmations with trust and gradually you will see a difference happening in whatever concerns you. The most effective time is first thing in the morning, when you are half-asleep, or last thing at night before you doze off.

There are many good books on the market that offer exercises to help you practice. Some titles are listed in this book's bibliography.

LOVE

Perhaps the most important ingredient in creating a prosperous life is love, not the romantic personal kind but universal, spiritual, unconditional love. I am going to go out on a limb again and suggest that we never really love anyone else — it's all reflected self-love. In other words, you cannot feel love for another if you don't feel it within yourself, for yourself. Rather than being selfish, this is a purer form of love because it is not co-dependent and does not come from need or self-serving motives. As we saw in the chapters on relationships, our reasons for falling in love and forming alliances often have little to do with love in its purer form. We often come together for dark, hidden motives that we're not even aware of.

When we're at peace with ourselves and we're 'complete' human beings, we naturally love everyone. You will never like everyone you meet but that should not preclude respect, compassion and tolerance.

By surrounding yourself with this depersonalised love, you will feel less pressured by close relationships and the demands they make on you. Some people will always be closer to you of course but you have enough love for everyone without preference or favouritism or jealousy.

I realise that I am speaking of a very idealistic concept but detachment does not mean not caring. It's simply removing the ego from relationships, loving everyone equally and being at peace with all differences and life styles and accepting everyone as your fellow human-being, no more and no less.

Since I have adopted this philosophy, I have entirely changed my view of personal relationships. It's very difficult for people who love me to understand what I mean, as naturally they feel I don't love them in a special way. In a sense that's correct but it also means I no longer demand to be special to them either. Love is a free-flowing energy and dies if it's defined or pinned down. Maybe that's why no-one has ever been able to say what it is. To me, it is a sense of joy and a life-force that you can feel surging through you. When you're in that space, you overflow with love and it automatically washes over everyone you meet. Haven't you ever met anyone who literally oozed love? You just want to be near them. That to me is charisma, not beauty or smooth talk or glamour.

When you love someone in the traditional sense, you usually want to be loved in return. To love unconditionally with no strings attached and without expectation is extremely difficult unless you can transcend your ego needs and love from your spiritual centre. As already said in the earlier chapters, romantic love is essentially an illusion and belongs more correctly in the pages of fiction. To love from your own well of joy and well-being is a gift that lasts because it does not depend on what the other person does or feels. A gift of love once given is given forever. You can never ask another person to love you in a particular way — it's an exercise in frustration; nor can you ask someone you love to stay with you, be it a child, a lover or a friend. Loving with open arms, without possession, is where it's at. If you think this is impossible, then look at how unsatisfactory is the way we've been doing it. Our divorce rates are horrific and even many people who stay together can't be happy. As the song says, we're 'looking for love in all the wrong places'. You have all the love you could ever need inside you and you can never be lonely, although in the strictest sense you are always alone.

You may not choose to spend time with a person you love if that person is a negative feature in your life; by the same token, you may choose to spend time with someone who is less close to you — these are choices that you can make. When you are involved in an intimate relationship that you want to be 'prosperous', you need only concern yourself with your half of the twosome. Be a loving person and hope your partner will want to share in that love. The same applies to happiness. It's a mistake to try and *make* someone happy. You will come up empty every time and both of you will suffer for it.

GIVING

We have all been taught that giving is an important part of being a good person. In this world, there are two types of people — takers and givers. Many women believe that they are in the latter category and men are all in the former. I don't believe that this issue is gender-based. There are givers and takers in both sexes. I would prefer to see both partners take turns as we all have revolving needs.

Neither way is preferable — it's only a problem when the giving and taking is out of balance and one-sided. Givers end up resentful and takers get lazy. Remember what was said earlier about playing out black and white roles. Give because you want to, not because you feel obliged or because you want to be loved in return.

If you don't nurture yourself, you will end up running out of energy and no-one will get anything more from you. Refill yourself, replenish, then you will spill over and the people around will actually get more, not less. Take time out for your own interests, see your friends, go out socially, spend money on yourself — if you're happy, you'll be a better husband and father anyway. Just remember moderation. It isn't self-love to booze away your money, spend all your time working or neglecting your family. Love also means consideration and caring.

Positive self-talk

- I know that happiness exists in the moment, in the here and now.
- I have power over my response to whatever happens to me, so I am never a victim.
- I 'follow my bliss'.
- I love unconditionally from my spiritual centre.
- I nurture and replenish myself, so I always have something to give.
- In any interaction I leave my partner with her own power, and I retain my own: a win situation.

Well, we've come to the end of a long road on which I have tried to put up signposts and leave you a map for the future. It is a map that leads to a treasure chest, not merely of material wealth: that can be lost or frittered away. This treasure is far more enduring. It will last your lifetime and beyond. It is the key to a happier, easier life. Many of the ideas and strategies I've shared with you I have only learnt myself in the past three years and many were hard won because, like you, I too had to shed many skins to get to my core. I am still only a seeker on my journey and have tons more yet to learn but, with the basic blueprint as my guide, I know I am always safe and can always find my way home if I should lose it.

If the main thing you gain from this book is the confidence to move past your fears and go searching for more joy in your life, I'll be glad. To find this treasure, you need not move away from your hearth and home for you have all the equipment you need within your heart, soul and mind.

Focus only on what you have right now, not on what you might have in the future, or what you lack. There is only abundance around you. Give thanks every day for what you have and what you want to get, for the latter is just as real if you believe it. There is no longer any need for 'if only' in your life, only the certainty of triumph.

When you start on this new journey, as I hope you will, you will meet many roadblocks and your resolve to change and evolve will be tested many times. Never see these as setbacks. It's your higher self testing you. Cry, scream, feel sorry for yourself, but the next day, get up, say your affirmations, follow your bliss, live your dreams and move forward, inch by inch if that's what it takes. Every time you face a challenge, you grow and strengthen.

I hope that many different types of men will read this book, not only the ones who are already on a spiritual path. You are all sacred and it doesn't matter whether you are religious or atheist or Buddhist or Christian. If anything I have said has offended, threatened or annoyed you, all the better — you now know where to focus your attentions. I am only your guide. You are the Master of your own destiny so give up pain, anger, violence, blame, addiction, conflict.

None of these is what it means to be human. Be free, be true to yourself, be unlimited. Walk towards the light of your own beauty; it's waiting for you.

I shall leave you with my favourite saying which sums up everything I have tried to say in this book: 'There is no way to happiness; happiness IS the way.'

BIBLIOGRAPHY

Bradshaw, John, *The homecoming*, Bantam Books, USA, 1992.

Broder, Michael, *The art of living single*, Wilkinson Books, Australia, 1988.

Coelho, Paulo, *The alchemist*, Harper San Francisco, 1994.

Dyer, Wayne, *Real magic*, HarperCollins, Australia, 1992.

Gawain, Shakti, *Creative visualisation*, Bantam Books, USA, 1982.

Gray, John, *Men, women and relationships*, Hodder Headline, USA, 1996.

Hay, Louise, *You can heal your life*, Hay House, USA, 1984.

Jeffers, Susan, *Dare to connect*, Random House, Australia, 1992.

Koran, Al, *Bring out the magic in your mind*, Thorsons, UK, 1972.

Lee, John, *Facing the fire*, Bantam Books, USA, 1990.

Montgomery, Bob, and Evans, Lynette, *Living and loving together*, Penguin Books, UK, 1995.

Ray, Sondra, *I deserve love*, Les Femmes Publishing, USA, 1976.

Redfield, James, *The Celestine prophecy*, Bantam Books, Australia, 1994.

Rowland, Michael, *Absolute happiness*, A Self-Communication Book, Australia, 1993.

Saunders, Charmaine, *Sex—Everything you want to know*, Sally Milner Books, Australia, 1995.

Scovel-Shiin, Florence, *The game of life*, Simon and Schuster, USA, 1986.